Praise for *Majesty*

Having written more than 600 hymns and choruses, Jack Hayford knows something about worship. *Majesty* explains how worship is a two-way interaction between God and man. While God is worthy of our worship and we are called to worship Him, Jack also explains the benefits *we receive* when we worship the Lord. If you want to know the Lord in a more intimate way, I highly recommend that you read this book.

ROBERT MORRIS
Founding Senior Pastor, Gateway Church
Bestselling Author of *The Blessed Life*,
Truly Free, and *Frequency*

Books like this one are very rare and this one is very important written by one of the world's greats, Dr. Jack Hayford. His wisdom, insight, leadership, and pastoral ability to shepherd a generation in the truth of a worshipful life will inspire you to the core. Your understanding will be increased as you read, as will your love of the Father. It is such an honour to add my endorsement to this life-changing book.

DARLENE ZSCHECH
Songwriter *Shout to the Lord* and Pastor

As a new Christian, no pastor was more influential to me than Jack Haytford. I attended his church for a year while completing my music degree. The priority he placed on worship and his practice of worship was a powerful example to me each week. Spirit-filled worship was followed by Sprit-filled, applicable teaching. This is an important book for everyone to read, especially anyone involved in worship ministry. Read it!

PAUL BALOCHE
World renowned worship leader,
Dove Award winning songwriter, and Author

MAJESTY

GOD ENTHRONED *in our* WORSHIP

JACK HAYFORD

GATEWAY CREATE PUBLISHING

Contents

Foreword

I HAVE MANY vivid memories from my years spent growing up in West Virginia. Several of those random snippets are happy recollections, some are simply fun and anecdotal, while others left a far more indelible mark on me—memories that shaped me and influenced my life's trajectory.

I remember how my mom and dad would usher my older sister, Jodi, and me into our family car every Sunday, and we'd make our way to our local Assemblies of God church. I recall how everyone in our congregation would raise their voices and sing out with all their hearts:

Majesty
Worship His majesty
Jesus who died, now glorified
King of all kings!

Little did I know then that I would one day have the privilege of getting to know the man who penned that song, which countless churches across the world have sung for over 40 years.

In the years since, Pastor Jack had made a tremendous impact on me—both directly and indirectly. I was first introduced to his writings when I attended Bible college because the curriculum included a few of his books. As time went on and I became a worship pastor, I really began diving deeply into the theology and significance of worship. It is during this time that I truly began to discover the treasure contained within his writings. Many of Pastor Jack's teachings and books have significantly shaped my understanding of worship.

However, Pastor Jack's heart for worship isn't confined only to the books, the teachings and the songs he writes; it's also very much a part of who he is and how he lives. Every time I've had the opportunity to be in a worship service with him, I've witnessed him worshipping with all of his heart and strength, arms outstretched in adoration of his heavenly Father. Pastor Jack's passion for worship is keenly evident in all that he says and does.

Whenever Pastor Jack visits Gateway Church, I love it when he and I can connect after a service. Sometimes he asks for sheet music for a particular song, while other times he tells me how a song personally ministered to him. He always makes an intentional effort to say something encouraging and affirming about the worship at Gateway.

Perhaps one of the most significant ways Pastor Jack has influenced my life comes from a story I once heard from him. Every Sunday night, he made a habit of walking around the sanctuary of his church in Van Nuys, California, laying hands on each seat, and praying for God's blessings on the people who would sit in them at the Sunday morning services. On one occasion, three other individuals joined him. They each went to a different corner and faced the center of the room with their hands extended in worship and prayer. Out of that experience, the Lord led Pastor Jack to Revelation 4, which speaks about the four living creatures who worship around the throne night and day. Ten days later, God gave him a vivid mental picture of the throne room of God descending and resting in alignment with the sanctuary of his church. One room blended into the other, with multitudes of heavenly hosts and earthly individuals raising their hearts in worship and praise to the One True King. From this, Pastor Jack came to a single conclusion: God is at work simultaneously in the visible and the invisible, in the physical and the spiritual, and a worshipping church stands at the heart of His reign. Why is this true? Because a church at worship is an expression of the power of the kingdom of God present now on earth, with the literal presence of God resting in the midst of the sanctuary.

As I heard Pastor Jack's story, he once again changed my perspective of worship. Every time we gather as a church in worship, I pray that God will rest in the center of our midst as our voices join with the saints, elders, and angels in giving Him the glory that He alone deserves.

However, Pastor Jack's life and teachings have not only personally influenced me and my understanding of worship; but they have also shaped the face of worship in the church as a whole today. Although he would humbly refuse to accept such a description about himself, I believe he is as equivalent to a modern-day Apostle Paul as anyone alive today. A glance back at his life, his ministry, and his legacy provides overwhelming evidence to this statement. Look beyond the large number of books he has written, the hundreds of songs he has composed, and his decades of faithful ministry, and you will find a man whose life is characterized by his deep, abiding passion to hear and obey God's voice through the Holy Spirit. The modern landscape of worship would look *very* different if it were not for him. He is truly a worship pioneer, and *Worship His Majesty* is his signature work on the topic.

Whether you're revisiting this classic book or experiencing it for the very first time, I believe God is going to speak to you. As you make your way through each chapter, I pray that you will absorb more than just information. I am asking God to make Pastor Jack's passion and heart for worship yours as well.

THOMAS MILLER
Executive Senior Pastor,
Gateway Church

Preface
The Meaning of Worship

IN A TROPICAL jungle, a man bows before a crude stick figure. In a fantastic Asian temple another burns incense before a richly decorated Buddha. A small group of people meets in an unobtrusive building in a small town in Nebraska to sing and pray together. Another man in the suburbs of Dallas spends the entire morning meticulously washing and waxing his foreign-made sports sedan. A teenage girl spends hours in her poster-plastered room listening to her favorite rock star.

All of these people are worshipping. In some cases, the worship is formal and easy to recognize. In others, we would generally hesitate to call it worship at all. However, everyone worships something or someone, and what you worship has a great influence on what you are—and what you will become.

Defining Worship

Man is a worshipper. Whether or not we acknowledge or recognize it, we all worship. Some people worship their jobs. Some worship money. Some worship possessions. Some people worship goals or desires. Some worship pleasure. Some of us even worship God!

Many people don't recognize what it is they worship because they don't have a clear idea of what worship means.

Understanding the meaning of worship is a good beginning place, because until we understand its meaning, we'll never understand its exercise.

Worship comes from the old English word *weorthscipe* and means "to ascribe worth unto." We'll look at this concept in depth later in the book, but the essential idea is that whatever it is that you value most highly, or give the greatest worth, is what you worship. You can see that people worship many different things, although we can justly say that worship rightfully belongs to God, for no one else can lay claim to the position of highest value in any person's life.

The Influence of Worship

Psalm 115 contains one of the most insightful statements on the subject of worship found anywhere in the Bible.

> Their idols *are* silver and gold,
> The work of men's hands.
> They have mouths, but they do not speak;
> Eyes they have, but they do not see;
> They have ears, but they do not hear;
> Noses they have, but they do not smell;
> They have hands, but they do not handle;
> Feet they have, but they do not walk;
> Nor do they mutter through their throat.
> Those who make them are like them;
> *So is* everyone who trusts in them (Psalm 115:4–8)

In this passage, the psalmist is talking about idolatry and the inadequacy of the idol gods the heathen worship. Then he makes a very important observation: those that make them are like them, and so is everyone who trusts in them. In other words, the Bible says, you become like the god you worship.

Let me say that again because I cannot overemphasize it: *you become like the god you worship.*

Worship means you are developing a set of values; you are determining what you desire most. Worship means you are choosing priorities; you are establishing what holds first place in your life. Worship means you are determining what you are to become; you are choosing in whose image you will be made. The gods that one worships begin to manifest their attributes in the worshipper. Therefore, in deciding what or whom to worship, you are also making decisions about your values and priorities, and how you should live.

The Issue of Worship

We see that some very significant issues arise from how we worship. Have you determined where you are going to bow? By bowing, I don't just mean a physical posture, but a stance of the soul. We bring our hearts into alignment with whatever we worship and we allow our hearts to begin to mirror that which we worship. Whom do you seek? What do you pursue? To what do you submit? The goal that you press toward—the object of your worship—will become the guiding force of your life.

Those who seek the Lord will find Him. They will discover the true purpose for which they were made and, ultimately, the fulfillment of that purpose. Those who follow another god will discover what that god provides, whether it is worry, decadence, or emptiness. J. B. Phillips has said there is a God-shaped vacuum in every one of us—a vacuum that only God can fill.

Worship is a way to fill that place inside us. Augustine said, "Lord, You've made us for Yourself, and our hearts find no rest till they find it in You." God created us for Himself, and the fulfillment of our hearts comes as a direct result of our approaching Him and coming to know Him. There can be no other fulfillment for that "God-shaped" place in us than the Lord Himself.

Finally, your worship will determine what flows from your life. Our highest attainment comes through glorifying Him who is worthy of all glory. Some may find temporary glory in their works or pursuits. Some may even be remembered beyond their lifetimes. But the one who worships the Lord—looking to the unseen rather than to the seen as we go through our present trials—will find what Paul calls an "eternal weight of glory" working in his life. That person will have a glory that endures.

God reveals Himself to those who bow before Him and seek Him. If with all your heart you truly seek Him, you will find Him. Then, when you discover what He's really like, glorifying Him will be the only natural response. Worship will lead you along that path.

Introduction

WE STOOD IN silent awe, sensing God's presence as shafts of sunlight arrowed through the gracefully arched windows high in the vaulted towers of the vacant abbey. The British countryside was welcoming another summer's morn as we ambled through the partially restored ruins of this ancient house of worship. Although it was disheveled and dilapidated, a dignity remained that was only a trace of the beauty it had known six centuries before at its dedication.

For two weeks, my wife Anna and I had been probing the corners of Scotland, Wales, and England in our tiny rental car, setting our own pace as we drove from place to place. We slowly grew accustomed to a left-hand-drive roadway system, but the caution and patience required by such unfamiliarity was not expediting our progress. So we chose a leisurely pace, visiting castles and cottages at our whim. Nothing dictated our schedule except that we were supposed to be at Oxford the third week of July. I was to participate in a conference there, studying the phenomenon of Spiritual Awakenings in a seminar under Dr. Edwin Orr's direction, following which we would return home to Los Angeles.

That summer the whole nation was enjoying a certain regal festivity as the people anticipated the silver anniversary of Elizabeth's coronation as Queen. It was amid this prevailing air of rejoicing in royalty that we were introduced to England.

Landing in Glasgow, after ten days of preaching in Denmark, we began our journey—sampling the variety of climates, customs, cuisine, and clothing styles from Inverness to Edinburgh to Llangollen to the Cotswolds. By the time we arrived in London, a special sense of wonder had overtaken us.

Occasionally I attempted to put into words the emotions I felt as history spoke to me at every turn. Whether we were quietly sitting in a park, reading an engraved plaque antedating us by centuries, strolling beside the Thames, or pushing our way through the crowds shopping at Harrods, an elusive sense of "the grand, the regal, and the noble" caught my imagination and defied my efforts at definition. However, on a side trip we made into Oxfordshire that definition came by surprise. It included a lesson I hadn't expected, and resulted in a song I hadn't sought.

It happened the day we drove to Blenheim.

Blenheim Palace is the massive estate built at Queen Anne's orders in the early eighteenth century. She presented it to John Churchill, the first duke of Marlborough, in honor of his leadership in the military victories against Spain. Two centuries later, Winston Churchill would be born and raised here, frequently retiring to this site for rest from the rigors of leadership during World War II. It was at Blenheim that he wrote many of his stirring speeches—speeches that inspired the English people to sustain their efforts at staving off Hitler's Luftwaffe, which was close to suffocating their will to survive.

A Person of Destiny

However, World War II was a full generation past, and we were walking through the spacious palace that had taken over eighteen years to build. It was after we passed outside and surveyed the sprawling grounds, so meticulously groomed and magnificently flowered, that the undefined feeling now surfaced and blossomed to a clear, complete thought. While overlooking the palace and grounds from the southwest and contemplating Churchill's former presence on the paths and fields, I mused aloud, "Being raised in such an environment would certainly make it far more credible for a person to conceive of himself as a person of destiny."

The idea effervesced within me. I seemed to have touched the nerve of a concept that had to do with far more than Blenheim and Churchill. It had first to do with that "something" Anna and I had felt these weeks as we traveled around Britain. However, it also extended to a fundamental issue of human nature—the grounds of self-worth and the purpose of human existence. All tied in together were unspoken questions and partial answers concerning how people perceive themselves and God's order of things. In some special way, there were traces of a larger and more complete pathway to discovering one's true identity and purpose—something realized in an undeclared, but real, national consciousness.

I'm not presuming that in one instant I plumbed the depths of a nation's psyche. However, I do feel that somehow my single observation began to explain a great deal of the spirit that permeates this small nation of such historic consequence. Here, only a generation ago, an outnumbered band, surpassed by superior technology, withstood the most sinister and vicious manifestation of evil in history. Motivating them was an inherent sense of righteousness, but driving the will to hold their ground was an awakened sense of destiny coupled with a historic sense of royalty as a clan.

Even as I stood there, millions of common folk of ordinary means were enthused and excited about celebrating one woman's royal ascent a quarter of a century earlier. This wasn't a case of idolatry, nor an instance of the mindless masses cowering before a ruling tyrant with no choice of doing otherwise. On the contrary, the people were rejoicing. The entire kingdom possessed a general mood of personal and national significance. It seems inescapably linked in some mystical way to the fact that each one perceives himself linked with, and personally represented by, the one who wears the crown and bears the scepter. To a visitor from another country, there seems to be a national dignity that flows to the general citizenry from the regal office of a single individual who reigns over them, exercising authority as an ennobled friend rather than as a feudal overlord.

Then a second thought exploded. This sense of dignity is the essence of the relationship Jesus wants us to have with His Church! He wants the fullness of His power, the richness of His nature, the authority of His office, and the wealth of His resources to ennoble our identity and determine our destiny!

Notwithstanding the deep emotion filling my soul, a holy calm and genuine joy possessed me. Standing there, my gaze sweeping the scene once again—the verdant, lush fields, the fragrance of roses everywhere, the magnificent architecture, with the stateliness of historic bearing—I gently squeezed Anna's hand.

"Honey, I can hardly describe to you all the things this setting evokes in me. There is something of a *majesty* in all this, and I believe it has a great deal to do with why people who lived here have been of such consequence in the shaping of history. I don't mean that buildings and beauty can beget greatness, but I do feel that some people fail to perceive their possibilities because of their dismal surroundings."

As we continued our walk, I spoke further of my concerns with which she agreed. She felt, as I did, a pastoral longing for people to understand the fullness of Jesus, to perceive His high destiny for each of them, and to see that our self-realization only comes through a realization of Him! How completely and unselfishly He invites us to become partners with Him in His Kingdom. He wants to transmit His Kingdom authority to us and through us as a flow of His life, love, and healing to a hopeless and hurting world.

Now something expanding and deepening that understanding was welling up within me. What had been undefined but sensed for more than two weeks of vacation journeying was now distilling into a single moment of awareness.

Majesty.

The word was crisp in my mind.

Majesty, I thought. It's the quality of Christ's royalty and Kingdom glory that not only displays His excellence, but that lifts us by His sheer grace and power, allowing us to identify with and share in His wonder.

Majesty.

As Queen Elizabeth's throne somehow dignifies every English citizen and makes multitudes of others partakers in a commonwealth of royal heritage, our ascended Savior sits enthroned and offers His regal resources to each of us.

Majesty.

As a nation rose against the personification of evil in the Nazi scourge, ignited to action by a leader who perceived himself a person of destiny created by a childhood identification with the majestic, so may the Church arise.

Kingdom authority.

"In my name they will cast out demons" (Mark 16:17), the King declared; and in going forth by the power flowing from His Throne, "the Lord working with *them*, and confirming the word through the accompanying signs" (Mark 16:20).

The crowds were increasing at Blenheim, and the marvel of the moment seemed no less real for becoming less intimate. "Let's go, honey," I said, and we started for the car. My soul was still resonating with the sound of a distant chord struck in heaven, but still a lost chord to much of the Church.

Worship His Majesty

As Anna and I drove along the narrow highway, the road undulating from one breathtaking view to another, I said to her, "Take the notebook and write down some words, will you, Babe?"

I began to dictate the key, the musical notes, the time value of each, and the lyrics (and she still insists that *she* wrote the song!):

> Majesty, Worship His Majesty!
> Unto Jesus be all glory, honor, and praise.
> Majesty, Kingdom authority,
> Flows from His Throne, unto His own,
> His anthem raise.
>
> So exalt, lift up on high the Name of Jesus.
> Magnify, come glorify, Christ Jesus the King.
> Majesty, worship His Majesty!
> Jesus who died, now glorified,
> King of all kings.

I completed neither the lyrics nor the music until weeks later, after we returned home. The piece was refined and edited over the piano in our living room, but the song was born in a moment as I envisioned the power of the majestic to transform a people and infuse them with a sense of significance and destiny.

At a time in history when more and more people lack this sense of worth, and at a time when the Church is uniquely equipped to address that emptiness, this song sounds forth a prophetic message:

> Rise, O Church, Worship His Majesty!
> Your strength is to stand before your King,
> For from His Throne all power in heaven and
>   earth flows unto His own who worship Him.
> He who died has ascended.
> Exalt Him, for in so doing He will exalt His own,
>   and make them triumphant in this their hour
>   of high destiny and purposed victory!
> Worship His Majesty!

The song has begun.

This book elaborates its meaning for all who sing it.

JACK W. HAYFORD

1

Reformation II

"He that has an ear to hear, let him hear what
the Spirit is saying to the churches."
Jesus

I propose we drive a nail in the altar.

Or the pulpit.

Or the communion table.

Or the organ bench ... or pipes.

Or the choirmaster's music stand.

Or any place both visible and sufficiently shocking to provide a counterpart to the ancient door at Wittenberg.

When Martin Luther nailed his 95 Theses to the university entryway, the sparks from his hammer ignited the Reformation.

A half-millennium ago, the Church was shaken to its roots—dragged by the nape of the neck to confront the reality of God's Word—and forced to face the fact that its forms had chained its people rather than freed them.

The Reformers trumpeted the dual truths of "justification by faith" and "the priesthood of the believer" and the true church—the people of God—was released through a recovery of the revelation of God's Word.

We're overdue for another one.

We might even ask if we are we in the earthquake throes of a new Reformation right now, even though we haven't defined its epicenter.

I think so. I think the twentieth century has been a hundred-year travail that is about to birth more than a Third Millennium. I believe we are about to see The *Church Glorious* emerge on the world scene.

I do not doubt that Christ could come again today. Whether He does or not, one thing is clear—the Holy Spirit already has come, and He's moving through the Temple and turning over tables. The surging waves of renewal's tide are flowing deeper and deeper until, today, the only place to escape is to flee to the high tower of traditionalism.

Trying to "Keep Control"

There is an unholy propensity in human nature to secure itself in history rather than open itself to simplicity—the simple touch of God, the summoning voice of the Spirit. Just as with the Reformation, ecclesiastical and theological resistance sustains its posturing against the new, the fresh, and the childlike. The effort to "keep control" breeds the forging of new instruments of doctrinal domination over the Church:

1. Simple openness to the Holy Spirit comes under assault as satanic because Pentecost's tongues occur again.
2. Suggestions that salvation's program intends to reinstate human dignity face a barrage of accusations of "humanism."
3. Applications of God's promises of blessing, health, and abundance may be either distorted or denounced, but any attempted, evenhanded welcome of both still falls under suspicion.

4. Proposals that new dimensions of prayer just might turn the day, and transform social and political institutions through intercession, are called presumptuous.

5. Proclamation of a bright hope for tomorrow, rather than the dismal prospect of defeat and deterioration, is said to smack of seduction.

6. A warmth of emotion, expressiveness, and spontaneity in worship are challenged as being fanatical, superficial, or insincerely casual.

These are but a few signs of voices "crying in the wilderness," calling for a preparing of the way of the Lord—the way for His Church moving into a new era. I have suggested many themes by the brief observations I've just made, but I am only dealing with one of them in this book.

A Reformation in Worship

I do not propose that this book is the counterpart to Luther's 95 Theses, but I would hope it might become one of 95 or more statements—a composite of calls from many quarters contributing to the new Reformation.

I want to underscore the reformation in worship that is in progress. This movement has already begun, and its fruit has been tested and proven worthy in a sufficient number of situations to show we are not simply dealing with a fad.

I do believe in the vision of The *Church Glorious*—the here-and-now unveiling of the Bride of Christ at a dimension of purity and power unknown heretofore. I *don't* believe in *triumphalism*—that pretend-world of the religious idealist who supposes that a band of super-saints will rise to take the earth by force and dominate society through supernatural power or political control. However, there is a *kingdom* to take and there is a *force* to exert, and the People of the Highest are the ones to do both.

Redefining, Unwrapping, Unsealing

I believe the pathway for the Church moving into its full destiny in God's counsels, while retaining a practical sanity and spiritual balance on earth's surface, lies in our perceiving the true purpose and spiritual dynamic in worship. For so long the Church has defined worship as an hour's exercise on Sunday, packaged by enculturated tradition, and preserved in doctrinarian posturing. Today, it is being *redefined, unwrapped,* and *unsealed.*

Worship is being *redefined* in terms of its form and focus. It isn't that we must scorn or discard valid traditions, but rather that newness must refill them with meaning. It isn't that we are trading objective adoration of God for a shallow subjectivism by worshippers. Rather, more people are discovering a simple, fulfilling intimacy as they praise Him.

Worship is being *unwrapped* in the removal of sectarian prejudices that have preempted interdenominational participation in biblical practices of worship heretofore labeled and shelved by feuding parties in the Body of Christ. Upraised hands are less and less a badge of the Charismatic and are becoming a simple sign of Christian praise. A learned appreciation for the dignity of liturgical life is increasingly finding a place among people who otherwise would have deemed it *lifeless.*

Worship is being *unsealed* as well. A theology of worship is coming into perspective that lends biblical dimension to the whole reformation process. The lid of traditional theology is being lifted. More are proposing worship as a dignifying, empowering act for *man*. Yet we are not seeking to make God man's servant. The historic approach to the doctrine of worship has focused so much on God, in an effort to verify His glory and underscore man's unworthiness that an unwitting surrender to "works" in worship has resulted. For example, the honest quest "to worthily worship God as He deserves to be worshipped," easily becomes performance-oriented and hermetically sealed against simple love, warmth, and emotion. The intellectual and artistic demands of religious duty may easily intrude upon the best intent of the worshipper, and suddenly we become those who "draw near to Me with their mouth, And honor Me with *their* lips, But their heart is far from Me" (Matthew 15:8).

The fruit of the Reformation of Luther, Calvin, Zwingli, Knox, and Huss' time was the unchaining of God's people. A new faith, *not* in church tradition, but in the Person of Jesus as the Justifying Savior, filled the hearts of millions. With that release—to stand conscience-free before the Judge of the Universe, look up into His face, and live in His peace—there came a new sense of destiny. The shackles of emotional, intellectual, and spiritual slavery were cast aside and a renaissance of learning and social advancement took place.

I believe a new Reformation in worship will accomplish the same thing. This comes at a time when the relevance of the Church is being challenged anew by an intellectually astute and technologically advanced—yet relationally disintegrating and spiritually thirsty—society.

An awakening to the power of worship to reinstate God's divine intent for man can answer contemporary questions of human purpose. A drug-drunk, suicide-prone, binge-oriented generation lives on that ragged edge because it has become dissipated by its empty affluence of information, experience, and pleasure. In the midst of everything, so few have anything, and the questions recur repeatedly: What are we here for? Why are things as they are?

This is not an exaggeration of the problem with people today, and neither is it an exaggeration to say that worship holds the solution to their dilemma.

The Bite in Worship

However, the Reformation breakthrough I propose will also require a confrontation with the tidiness of our systems. Just as Luther's voice provoked existing religious structures, so it seems to irritate some today when the neatness of prescribed worship ideas and methods are confronted with fresh approaches and new insights. The "bite" in worship presses in, calling for the sacrifice of everything in us that seeks to secure itself in humanly devised systems of thought and practice. This "bite" calls us to move from our presuppositions into an honest confrontation with worship's foundational requirement: sacrifice.

Sacrifice has always been involved at the heart of all worship of the Most High God. It is the "bite" in worship. By "bite," I mean the cost—and the price is usually blood. Blood, that is, as in *life*—the laying down of what we scream to preserve or spare in our own interest.

With Abel, it meant an animal's blood.

With Abraham, it meant circumcision.

With Israel, it meant the Passover.

With David, it meant exuberance.

With Ezra, it meant confrontation with opposition.

With Jerusalem's multitudes, it meant palms and shouting.

With Pentecost's participants, it meant supernatural praises.

With Paul, it meant singing with grace in his heart.

With Peter, it meant a completely new priestly order involving *you*.

In every case, there was—there *is*—a "bite" in worship, a price that confronts the cultural tastes of man. As much as we want beauty and as beautiful as worship may be, with God beauty is always secondary—life precedes loveliness. He resists whatever obstructs that life, no matter how "beautiful" the human option may appear.

Cain preferred the beauty of the bloodless.

Society mocked the mutilation of Abraham's "mark."

Egypt scorned the bloody doorposts of the Hebrews.

Michal was disgusted with her husband David's dancing to God.

Ezra's spiritual warfare-unto-worship crowds our religious comfort zone.

The Pharisees would rather have a more orderly Triumphal Entry—if one at all.

The analysts of Pentecost determined that the worshippers were drunk.

Paul's song was reduced to a form rather than released in the Spirit.

Peter's sanctuary of "living stones" has become petrified in tradition.

Tradition.

We love it and we hate it. We would die for it, but we can't live with it. Its role in worship is pervasive; tradition has shaped no part of human experience more than the way we worship. Even in the Body of Christ, frequently the force of tradition overrides the truth of God's Word. Whether we like to acknowledge it or not, we prefer worship styles that suit taste and tradition *first*, and the truth is often secondary where worship's demand, or "bite," is concerned.

Discerning between the principles of worship and the practice of worship is the demanding challenge we face. To do so is to risk discarding our security blanket of warm and fuzzy feelings about worship and to press for the fashioning of a new wardrobe of priestly garments. As with any wardrobe, we need a pattern to follow.

A Pattern of Pursuit

"To Him who loved us and washed us from our sins in His own blood, and has made us kings and priests to His God" (Revelation 1:5–6).

These words supply a pattern for our quest of reformed and refined worship. First, this pattern exalts the *Person* we worship— Jesus, who died to redeem us from sin's curse of eternal death, and who did so at the expense of His own lifeblood shed on the Cross.

Second, it qualifies the *practice* of our worship—a priestly ministry, providing the reminder that worship involves the priestly traits of *duty* and *purity*. The lessons of Israel's priesthood teach us well. Having been made priests unto our God and Savior, we have a lifelong *call* (one never outgrows worship) and a holy *calling* (purity and piety are not options).

Third, it presents the *perspective* on worship: Kingship!

In one verse we are shown how He who has (1) washed us from our sins, and (2) made us priests unto God, has accomplished yet a third thing as well—He has made us *kings* under the King of kings. More literally, the text describes us as a kingdom of priests, or in Peter's words, "a royal priesthood." Nevertheless, Peter uses the majestic imagery of courts and kingdoms and of regal pomp and circumstance to describe us. Though it may fit few of us from *our* viewpoint of ourselves, we must still deal with this fundamental thread of thought portraying royal imagery. It's at the heart of grasping His Majesty's call to worship Him as *kings* as well as priests. Kings have to do with *ruling*, with *kingdoms*, with *authority*, and, very often, with *warfare*. Too seldom, we have seen worship as related to spiritual warfare and conquest. Worship should introduce God's Kingdom power throughout the Church and extend that power *through* the Church.

Kingdom authority is the issue.

The worship of Christ should show itself in more than aesthetic brilliance or doctrinal excellence. It should distill the authority of Jesus among and upon the lives of the worshippers, to infuse their lives so that it might influence everything *they* influence.

The bottom line is *Kingdom authority.*

Majesty, Worship His Majesty!
Unto Jesus be all glory, power, and praise.

Majesty, Kingdom authority,
Flows from His Throne, unto His own,
His anthem raise.

It is the *Reformation I* perspective of this hymn that *all* praise and worship are due to God's Son, "Jesus who died, now glorified, King of all kings," who alone is the Lord of our salvation and the One Mediator between God and man. But it is also the *Reformation II* perspective of this hymn that God's worship plan ushers in a present release of His power—an operational dimension of His love and life—"in the midst of all who worship Him in spirit and truth."

A reformation in worship will apply its "bite." Reformations do that—pressing against any resistance of human pride, and pushing us past any personal preoccupation with our "warm fuzzies."

2

It Was Meant
to Be So Different

"Every valley shall be exalted And every mountain and
hill brought low ... The glory of the Lord shall be
revealed, and all flesh shall see *it* together ..."
Isaiah 40:4–5

RICHARD AND MICHELLE's baby died.

It was a case of crib death or SIDS—that unexplained, invisible suffocator of infants. Besides being devoted parents, they were also faithful servants to the congregation where they labored as pastoral assistants. Now, with the baby's death, a cluster of questions was buzzing overhead like flies, as various local people, hearing of the tragedy, probed one another with the usual questions:

"Where is God when things like this are happening?"

"They're such a sweet couple. What did they do to deserve this?"

"Why does God allow these things? After all, the little thing was so helpless."

"She was such a sweet baby. How will they handle the pain?"

Richard and Michelle didn't have any such questions. Only tears.

Grief was deeply and understandably present, but so was a warm, very human, and unpretentious simplicity of faith. They knew Kirstin's death had nothing to do with God. He neither willed her death, nor took her life, nor did He watch the passing of their child with indifference.

Within their sorrow, and undiluted by their tears, a quiet confidence reigned. Its rule was one that prevails when people understand that such situations are neither God's will nor God's fault—that tough things happen because our planet is sadly out of joint with God's intended order of things. They knew the facts that pertain to humankind's forfeited rulership of a world entrusted to them by the Creator, and the problems of a world now "on its own" by humanity's own willful decision. They knew the truth that people have become painfully vulnerable to the consequences of a lost government—a maverick unpredictability now prevailing all too often. They knew that in His original design God meant everything to be so different.

Richard and Michelle discovered these truths in learning to worship.

Through their years of preparation for ministry, they had grown in Christ and in understanding. They had grown in a pattern of giving and serving in Jesus' name. Their baby's death staggered them, but they didn't stumble. At the root of their stability was a steadfastness that was neither feigned nor forced. There was a solid perspective on "man-as-he-was-meant-to-be." The role of worship in all this was foundational and essential. For at its core, worship is not a kind of church service so much as an understanding of life: how to rule in life rather than being ruled by it, even when tragedy strikes.

The Primal Tragedy

Most people who know the Bible perceive that the presence of all the adversity in our world dates to the primal tragedy—the fall of man from his first estate in creation's order. The opening pages of Scripture succinctly set the stage for our understanding of God's loving plan of recovery for our race. God's Word describes the reason for the human dilemma. The biblical record of (1) creation's perfect and original order, (2) man's intended destiny, and (3) the fouling of them both, does more than merely place blame. This record of failure also introduces hope. It establishes the foundation of purpose and promise for our lives by introducing us to *worship*.

At the root of God's revelation to us, worship is the prerequisite for man's living within the high possibilities and rich benediction of God's plan. Even though the opening chapters of Genesis set forth worship as the foundation for building a successful life, I hadn't seen this truth before.

I traced my blindness on this perspective to an inadequate explanation I had been given for man's creation—the widely quoted and generally accepted half-truth that "God created man for fellowship." Christians so glibly repeat that statement in general, that one might think it was in the Bible. Yet it's only a fraction of the *whole* truth and it's drastically less than what the Creator had in mind when He created man.

Of course, "fellowship" with God is a rich part of the privilege granted to humans. Nevertheless, there is an underlying shallowness to the proposition that fellowship was God's sole or primary purpose in making us. It somehow presents the picture of a lonesome deity who conjures up creatures to insure that He will have friends present at His weekend parties. The Bible teaches differently. It clearly reveals that God was creating people not so much for "fellowship" as He was establishing them for "rulership"—granting us a relationship with our Creator, which could insure us the ability to carry out our intended role, to become *rulers*.

Created for Rulership

When the Three-in-One determined, "Let us make man in Our image," He gave the reason: "Let them [man] have dominion" (Genesis 1:26). The realm of our dominion was to be all the earth, and God's purpose, while including fellowship, was definitely more than that. God was inviting us into *partnership* with Him. He was making us kings.

The dimensions of God's and our domains were greatly different. God was and is *The* Creator and *The* Ruler of the entire Universe, whereas He created us to be rulers of one planet (Psalm 115:16). But there is no escaping this awesome fact: God, without jealousy for His own power and at great risk in potential cost to Himself, not only created a being with certain capacities much like His own, but He welcomed that creature into a kind of co-regency, at least insofar as earth was concerned. The privilege of rulership was our role, but resource for its performance depended upon a foundational *relationship*; we would sustain our rule by worshipping Him. The Creator-creature relationship made worship appropriate, and our finite resources mandated it. It was so at the beginning. It is so today.

He who first wakened unto his being, looking into the face of the One who had just breathed existence into him, knew beyond question the source of his life. *Thanksgiving* for his being prompted His worship.

He who stood upright as no other creature and who could gaze beyond the horizon of his earth-home to behold the stars, intuitively knew the heavens beyond were the handiwork of the same One who had formed his physical frame. *Humility* and *awe* at the Creator's power were added worship themes.

He who received the first commandments—be fruitful, multiply, replenish the earth, subdue it, and exercise dominion—was sensitized to yet another reality: "Awesome powers have been entrusted to me." Acknowledged *dependency* responded to the magnanimity that shared such power.

He who heard the sole restriction upon him, "but of the tree of the knowledge of good and evil you shall not eat" (Genesis 2:17), perceived his finiteness and his accountability to One wielding infinitely higher authority. Knowing that *obedience* is the conclusive and ultimate response true worship requires, man the worshipper obeyed.

For how long man walked with God in this relationship founded on worship, daily responding with thanksgiving, humility, awe, dependency, and obedience, we do not know. However, there was an unblemished era of obedience when man, the worshipper of God, partnered with the Almighty as man, the ruler. He tasted the delight of complete fulfillment, broad authority, wide possessions, and personal significance. Within the circle of a relationship that released his highest potential, he *also* enjoyed a companion-like fellowship with the Almighty One, his Maker.

And then man fell.

Man violated the one condition on which rested the joy derived from his relationship and his rulership. When Adam disobeyed, he severed the bond of obedient worship. He no longer worshipped in the spirit of thanks, humility, awe, and dependency. His relationship with the Creator was broken. His pristine dignity was lost and his authority for rulership surrendered. Because the damning act had been the result of obeying the serpent's lie, he had both yielded his trust and forfeited his rule to the tempter.

This double tragedy of the *loss* of man's rule under God *and* its *displacement* into the gnarled claws of the dragon, constitutes the basic explanation for the tragic—the deadly, the destructive, and the damning—as it wreaks havoc upon our world.[1] What was lost through the violation of worship's proper order seemed hopelessly gone. However, God's Word immediately introduces hope. The Creator is about to disclose a plan by which man can regain the purpose God intended for him. It will involve the reinstatement of man by reestablishing pure worship.

Beginning the Reinstatement

The wonder of God's wisdom lies not so much in His power to create as in His power to redeem.

Genesis 3 is both the foundation of man's horror and the fountainhead of his hope. God's love and wisdom shine forth in the speed with which He confronts the disaster sin has introduced to the race. He immediately sets forward two things—a *promise* and a *provision*—for mankind's redemption. Only divine wisdom can move so quickly, cover so thoroughly, deal so consistently, and love so graciously.

Launching a program of forgiveness and redemption violates nothing of God's foundational order. With one stroke, God deals with man's fallenness with both justice and mercy. He confronts the sin and administers specific judgment on each party involved, then turns to solve the long-term need of the lost pair.

There is a holy determination to recover all that He intended. The Father insists that hell's plot will not destroy man's destiny. The Almighty One has already addressed the serpent. He will eventually strike a conclusive blow. A Redeemer-Seed will be born who will break the power Satan has seized (Genesis 3:15). However, with this promise He unfolds a provision for the two who stand before Him—ashamed, bereft of former glory, severed from God, and stripped of the ruling power He gave them.

While the brevity of the Genesis record does not relate the conversation that followed, let us not make the mistake of supposing too much or too little from the text: "Also for Adam and his wife the Lord God made tunics of skin, and clothed them" (Genesis 3:21). Few words report the provision made for clothing the couple, and I'll not suggest that He gave an elaborate outline of redemption's plan. However, we do know one thing: they understood that offering a sacrifice was more than a means for clothing. It instituted the path of worship by which they would realize their recovery.

The evidence of their understanding is confirmed in the following chapter. God taught fallen man the significance and substance of his worship—his offerings to God. That is why Abel obediently practices the worship that his parents taught him. That is why Cain—fully aware of what God expects in worship and fully warned not to violate the pattern he also had learned—is judged so sharply (Genesis 4:1–7). The issue is crucial, and it is also clear—worship was the foundation of man's being and potential. Worship is the foundation of God's redemptive program.

There is an impressive symmetry in this. Man's relationship and rule under God had been rooted and sustained in worship. Now, just when both seem to be irretrievably lost, God sets forth a recovery plan. With unsurprising consistency, yet with an amazing simplicity, this plan also centers on worship!

There is no show of power.

No display of cosmic almightiness.

No instant smashing of the serpent.

No fury leveled at the guilty.

Instead, there is an introduction to a humble act of worship. The Redeemer's grace seems to exceed even His power as He sets forth to recover for His beloved creature all that has been lost. Yet the program is not as one might expect, for its hidden power is in the reinstatement of worship rather than in a demonstration of might. The mightiness will flow from worship.

Lost and Restored

Obedience would have been better than sacrifice; however, what *dis*obedience lost, sacrifice restores!

The slain animal whose skin provided clothing for the glory-stripped couple forecasts how the coming of the Seed would vanquish the snake. For the promise just given was that moment being fulfilled in part. What the serpent had done in breaching a relationship, God was undoing in the sacrificial provision—His forecast of an ultimate annulment of the evil power that had intruded into the divine order. A sudden leaping of the centuries and we see so clearly the amazing consistency in God's order. The same issue is present in the desert as in the garden. When the Seed and the snake have their first head-on encounter, the issue is still relationship and rulership. Worship is the summons and world-rule is at stake:

> Again, the devil took Him up on an exceedingly
> high mountain, and showed Him all the kingdoms
> of the world and their glory. And he said to Him,
> "All these things I will give You if You will fall down
> and worship me." Then Jesus said to him, "Away

with you, Satan! For it is written, 'You shall worship
the Lord your God, and Him only you shall serve.'"
(Matthew 4:8–10).

This precise symmetry is foundationally important to our
whole understanding. Worship will only make *complete* sense
when we understand its place in God's *complete* plan. He did not
give worship as a test of will but as the source of our potential.
He has not created man as a pawn or a plaything, but to become
a partner in His highest purposes.

Just as *defiled* worship broke man's relationship and forfeited
his dominion, *restored* worship can redeem both relationship and
rulership. God's forgiveness of our sin establishes relationship,
and His reinstating our intended purpose promises rulership.
God offers man both deliverance from evil and dominion over
it—a continual walk with God and growing triumph over hell.
As in the beginning when the foundations for man's life—his purpose and fulfillment—were laid in worship, so redemption's program seeks to reinstate man by restoring those foundations. Jesus
Himself has established a new beginning point for perfect worship. He is the sacrifice. He is the High Priest. He is the leader in
worship—restoring any member of Adam's race who will return
to relationship with God. However, restored relationship through
reestablished worship is not the sum of the redemption plan. The
full scope of the divine program of retrieval is broader.

God intends to restore man's rulership as well: "Repent, for
the kingdom of heaven is at hand" (Matthew 4:17). Repentance
is, in essence, the renewal of worship. Because repentance resub-
mits us to God's rule again, two lost possibilities reappear: the
resurrection of our relationship *with* Him and the restoration of
our rulership *under* Him. Our return to our intended place of
obedient worship not only places us *under* God's Kingdom rule

again, it also makes possible a reinvestment of that rule among humankind.

Our full understanding of worship's potential for our life is diluted if we miss this point. Just as relationship was *not* the sole purpose of our *creation,* so our recovery is *not* the sole purpose in our *salvation.* We were created for rulership as well, and full salvation includes the restoration of that *rule*—dominion, authority, creative responsibility, and accountability. While the fullest implications of that restored rule will not be clear until the eternal future, God calls believers *now* "to reign in life"—to begin relearning the dimensions and the exercise of the dominion that God originally granted. In our present lifetime, growth in this plan begins and extends as we learn that worship is the way to all rulership being exercised and all dominion being expanded (Matthew 5:17).

What Rule? What Dominion?

What are the implications of restored rule—of renewed dominion? The words seem so towering, so potentially "high and mighty." However, the issues are intensely practical and related to the basics of everyday living. This is important, because it is exactly *there* that so many believers who have *relationship* with God seem to fail to regain rulership. By looking at what sin lost, we can better understand what we might regain:

1. Man lost his righteous relationship with God—evidenced by his awareness of his nakedness and his flight from God's presence (Genesis 3:7–11).
2. Man lost his healthy relationship with his spouse—evidenced by accusation and alienation between them, and

by family strife between their children later (Genesis 3:12, 16, 20; 4:8).

3. Man lost his ability to deal effectively with his environment—evidenced by the fact that his "workplace" came under a curse, reducing yield and thereby his relative success (Genesis 3:17–19).

4. Man lost his promise of life—evidenced by the entry of disease, depression, and death, and, apart from redemption, eternal destruction (Genesis 2:17; 3:19).

To summarize, man lost (1) confidence in his relationship with God, (2) the ability to rule well in his own household, (3) his fruitfulness and effectiveness in his vocation, and (4) his certainty of hope for a life of physical, mental, and emotional health.

In light of that summary of loss, the Word of God opens the way to an understanding of the practical dimension of dominion we can expect to regain through worship:

1. *Dominion over condemnation:* Worshipping opens the heart to perceive God's love and grace in a growing way. My full acceptance in Christ's righteousness establishes a foundation of confidence for living.

2. *Domestic order:* Husband-wife and parent-child relationships begin to change for the better in homes where the spirit of praise and the simple, loving worship of God prevail.

3. *Economic freedom:* A person's ability to succeed in work and advance in his financial situation is verifiable repeatedly where the principles of worship-with-finance are applied (i.e., stewardship and giving).

4. *Personal wellness:* The praiseful person is destined to be healthier simply because the human physical system

responds positively to such a prevailing mental and emotional attitude.

What defiled worship lost, God's program of revived worship in Christ can restore! This is what a growing number of people are discovering today. As they are experiencing a revival in worship, a renewed sense of God's rule is coming into their lives. It's a biblical principle: where God can find people who will worship *within* His will, He extends His Kingdom rule *through* them. "For the eyes of the Lord run to and fro throughout the whole earth, to show Himself strong on behalf of *those* whose heart *is* loyal to Him" (2 Chronicles 16:9).

Admittedly, there is a delicate balance here.

We can be sure of some restoration in all the above "losses" that fallen man experienced, but God's Word gives us no guarantee of perfection in any respect until the complete restoration of all things in His *future* Kingdom.

There is a *presence* of His Kingdom authority bequeathed to His own *now*, however. Let none of us forfeit the present dimensions of "Kingdom authority" by not pursuing the recovery of His rulership in our lives. Let us not fear beginning that pursuit, feeling disqualified by our failures in the past or by our present sense of weakness. It isn't a presumptuous thing for a saved sinner to expect.

How do we begin that pursuit?

We should not be surprised to find that worship is the key at every point! As we walk in the Holy Spirit-power of worship, we can recover life as God meant it to be. We can receive all the fullness that salvation has for us as we rebuild the foundations of worship that God first gave to man: "When we keep looking at Jesus with a real openness to the Holy Spirit's ministry, we will begin to brightly reflect the beauty of Christ and keep becoming like Him" (2 Corinthians 3:18 author's paraphrase).

Worship recovers all that Adam lost. It is God's way for each of us to find a progressively restored dominion in our lives.

There is no dimension of Adam's loss that may not be recovered now in Christ.

Even the dimension of death changes.

First, God promises us the hope of eternal life, certified with hard evidence—the resurrection of our Lord Jesus Christ! Nevertheless, we all still have an appointment with death (Hebrews 9:27). Not even restored worship can recover immortality in this world. Contrary to the opinion of a few sincere souls, no one can commandeer a certain date or insure a certain lifespan.

However, whenever death does touch us through the passing of one we love, the spirit of understanding in worship transforms the moment. Though tears may fill our eyes, dominion has returned to our souls. The true worshipper is not ruled by death, its force, or its fear—he has dominion over it.

Ruling in Life

That dominion prevailed with Richard and Michelle when baby Kirstin died. Two days after the baby died, Michelle was looking at the small body in the tiny casket, with her pastor's wife, Becki, standing by her side. The bereaved mother smiled slightly. In a quiet yet strong voice, she spoke:

"You know, Kirstin, I thought you were going to be with me all my life. I thought we'd bake cookies together and I thought you would wear my wedding dress. But you were only going to be here a short time, and I didn't know that."

Then Michelle turned to the woman beside her. Becki's arms had slipped around Michelle's waist, and her eyes had filled with the tears of a mother who understands. Then Michelle said:

"Becki, I really only have one thing to say. It's been worth it all. Kirstin has brought Richard and me so much joy in the short time we had her. I cannot be anything but thankful."

She paused. "And you know what, Becki? I can hardly wait to get pregnant again."

Worship is for people—people of Adam's race—whom Jesus Christ is teaching to recover the lost dominion God meant us all to have. Things may not always be as God intends. Before the foundations crumbled under sin's destructive blow, life was meant to be so different. However, just as worship could have preserved man's foundation for dominion, worship can restore whatever dimensions anyone wants to learn and rebuild.

Richard and Michelle learned well.

The question we face together—looking at worship's intended possibilities for restoring man's created role of *ruler*—is whether we're ready for the new reformation unto which it calls.

3

Worship Is for People

"But John's father told him the Steward would be
angry if he did not sit absolutely still and be very good;
and John was beginning to be afraid, as he sat in the
high chair with his feet dangling, and his clothes itching
all over him, and his eyes staring out of his head"
C. S. Lewis from *The Pilgrim's Regress*

I WASN'T TUNED in yet to a reformation or to a concept of
worship as a means to releasing rulership. I was, however,
ready to challenge the "warm fuzzies" of my own worship tradition. Though I didn't know it, a phenomenal development
in my understanding of worship was about to take place.

It all began with a conversation in an elevator.

The Academic Dean of the College was asking me to teach
a course very unacademically and uncleverly named *Song
Direction*. I didn't like the idea. In fact, I didn't like anything
about the course as it was structured. It seemed to focus on
church worship services as perfunctory duty and on church
platform leaders as keepers of the machinery of worship.

"Why do you want me to teach it?" I complained. "I really
don't want to. There are lots of other faculty who can handle
it at least as well as I could."

"That's just the problem, Jack. No, there aren't."

I was flattered, at least until the Dean continued, "Virtually no one else's fall schedule can accommodate the time frame opened for the class, and yours does. Besides, you have a natural gift for music and—well, you're also a composer, and ...."

I don't know exactly how the sentence ended. I was trying to overcome the scuttling of my flattered feelings, finding that my primary qualification for selection was simply my schedule. Nevertheless, the minor lacerations to my pride had been salved somewhat by the allusion to my limited musical skills, and when the new semester opened, I was on the spot.

I had accepted the assignment on the terms that I could restructure the course. The Dean approved my syllabus, and we changed the name to "'Introduction to Worship."

Song Direction was a required class, so the sophomore students were trapped. As they filed in the first day, I could see that their conversations with experienced upperclassmen had not filled them with expectation. However, as we began to take a fresh look at worship, the dread turned into excitement.

The basis of our examination of worship could be expressed in one basic question: "What are church services supposed to be about?"

That question spawned a seemingly endless series of others, such as:

"Why do we sing in church?"

"Why are 'services' called that?"

"'What are the scriptural grounds for the actions and activities that comprise our services?"

"What is 'liturgy'? Do only liturgical churches have 'liturgies,' or do we *all*?"

"What practices do we observe that have become mere formalism or dead habit? Why do you think they're like that? How did they get that way?"

However, while questioning various worship practices, I cautioned the students to resist an attitude of judgmental criticism or smug snobbishness. "After all," I said, "it is worship we're assessing, so let's operate from this premise: any wearying habit or dead tradition that we note in our churches was probably good at the start."

That approach did wonders, and I still recommend it to people seeking renewal in their church traditions. When any of us search for the valid reasons our traditions may have had at their inception, we should do so with a humble, seeking heart and a sympathetic spirit of hunger for truth. That prayerful attitude will contribute toward the refreshing we want. Therefore, we set out to find what generated "spiritual life forms," when and how they were born, and what biblical grounds supported or interpreted those various practices.

A Refocused Viewpoint

The result was successful, academically speaking, but beyond that, our quest proved to be experientially rejuvenating. Something started vibrating in the class as the students began to tune in to a real spirit of revival. It was much more than I had hoped for. Even the "song leading" drill began to throb with life. We had gone beyond analysis to application, for in sensitively discussing what a service was supposed to be, we gained a perspective on a two-edged truth I had never defined before. A worship service should:

- Serve God with our praise
- Serve people's need with His sufficiency

That one sentence refocused worship for me.

My orientation and approach had been primarily toward a

single purpose in church services: we gather to worship God. Now, without supplanting the worship of God, we were adding a second focus: man's need and God's ability to supply it. We deduced that worship is to be *to* God and *for* man. For me, that simple statement brought a new insight into the classic definition of human purpose so frequently quoted from the Westminster *Shorter Catechism*: "The chief end of man is to glorify God and to enjoy Him forever." I was surprised—the dual emphasis had been there all the time, but I hadn't seen it. The Catechism's words had always seemed to strike my ear as exalted and high sounding. While "to glorify God" is obviously a worthy endeavor, the sum of "to enjoy Him forever" seemed distant— reserved only for the heavenly future.

Suddenly, to my delight, I saw this classically approved and theologically acceptable statement declaring the same dual truth we were learning about worship. First, God *is* to be the focus of our praise. Second, He had *always* planned that in worship we would find joy, blessing, fulfillment, and purpose.

There was a simple but fresh touch of life in this discovery.

Indeed, we concluded that worship is for people, and another dual set of observations crystallized the idea.

Tests: Reason and Revelation

There were two tests to apply to our discovery. The first had to do with human response, and the second with biblical truth.

First, I proposed we examine the elements that comprised most of our worship services. If worship is for people, and if God meant it to restore them, then why are people so often more bored than blessed? What did we need to do to reverse our viewpoint from worship as "requirement" to worship as "opportunity"? I looked at the basics. I was convinced that the practices of worship were designed to fulfill people, and I wanted to overcome any attitude diminishing that potential for joy. We looked at several worship "mandates."

"Assemble yourselves together" (Hebrews 10:25). Could it be that God calls people *together* to worship Him, and *not* to cause inconvenience? Could it be that He calls us *together*, not because worship can't take place in private, but because we have so much potential for fulfillment when we come together in the spirit of His love? On the contrary, however, if our "gathering" is merely by constraint, motivated by guilt, or packaged for the institution rather than for the individual, then worship will soon dissolve to drudgery or slavery.

Many people excuse themselves from their accountability to worship by saying, "I worship God all the time, in whatever I'm doing." That's good. We should allow everything we do to be glorifying to Him, but we also have a need for regular times of concentrated worship with other believers. We need to experience the refreshing at the soul level that comes from worship and fellowship. Hebrews 10:25 tells us this will become all the more important as we see the day of His glorious return approaching.

"Sing unto the Lord" (Psalm 96:1). There are 85 places in the Bible where we are directed to sing. Could it be that God calls people to *sing* their worship to Him, not because He's intent on increasing their cultural awareness or musical skills, but because singing is a natural expression of human joy and love? On the contrary, however, if song is removed from declaring insights, testimonies, and exaltation of God's goodness, it will become less than rejoicing, and stodginess or dreariness will take over.

God's Word repeatedly and directly tells us that singing releases joy. It's easy to sing when the joy of the Lord fills our hearts, but the Bible says to do it at other times too. Studying the Psalms, we see David singing to the Lord in the middle of some difficult situations. The song he sings isn't always, "He has put a new song in my heart, even praise unto our God." Some of David's songs say, "There are people after me, God! Protect me; be my shield." In other psalms, he expresses confession or sorrow. It becomes clear that it is with more than a subjective point of excitement that we sing. It's something the Lord has said to do because singing release power. Even when we don't feel like it, and even when it may not be very exciting at a particular juncture in our lives given the circumstances, it is wise to lift our voices to praise Him and worship Him with song.

"Continuing in prayer, sharing, and the apostles' doctrine" (Acts 2:42). Here is a cluster of three worship practices, all of which allow the prospect that God meant them to fulfill *us* as we worshipped Him. They all are *openings* to divine possibilities for us.

Prayer

The language of worship is found in prayer. Psalm 65:2 says, "O You who hear prayer, To You all flesh will come."

The Lord does hear prayer and we offer our prayer in many different ways. All of them are full of worship in this respect: they are brought into submission to Him. The Lord's Prayer concludes, "Yours is the kingdom and the power and the glory forever. Amen" (Matthew 6:13). That's the worship summary statement concerning our prayer—everything is His.

Let's look at a few aspects of prayer and how they speak to the language of worship:

1. *Confession.* Although gross sin may not have been a part of our lives, we need to come simply before God each day and say, "Lord, I'm growing in Your ways, but I'm not

there yet. Forgive my shortcomings and continue to shape me into Your image."

2. *Petition.* We all face needs for help, provision, strength, healing, and wisdom. However, we may also inquire, "Lord, what would You have me do? How would You have me direct the details of my life? I submit them to You and in all my ways acknowledge You, that You may direct my paths."

3. *Praise.* The Psalmist says that we are to "enter into His gates with thanksgiving, and into His courts with praise" (Psalm 100:4). Offering praise to the Lord is not only a means of accessing His throne, but is also an appropriate way to remember His goodness every day. Then, stepping into His presence, we wait there to receive direction from our living God.

4. *Meditation.* This is not some transcendental trip or a superstitious, mystical exercise. Meditation is to think upon what the Lord has said and wait on how He will speak to me through His Word and by His Spirit.

5. *Intercession.* It is the great privilege and responsibility of believers to agree with the Almighty for the invasion of His force and His might into any situation where the press of circumstance, judgment, or the attack of the enemy is coming down on people. For example, Paul directs us to pray for our governmental leaders and all who are in authority "that we may lead a quiet and peaceable life in all godliness and reverence" (1 Timothy 2:2).

6. *Adoration.* We are commanded to exalt Him and to adore Him who is worthy. The Psalmist says, "Exalt the Lord our God, and worship at His footstool—for He is holy" (Psalm 99:5).

The language of worship is sensible. Prayer is man glorifying the living God and, in these ways, coming appropriately before His throne in a sane, sensible, responsible exercise of worship.

Preaching

This is a time for the opening of His Word, designed to inspire and uplift, to stir faith, and to beget hope. Preaching that only informs without inspiring, or that only confronts without instilling hope, may be orthodox, but it may also be counterproductive.

Long ago, Jesus, just prior to His ascension, met with the Twelve as they gathered in Galilee. There they worshipped Him. "And Jesus came and spoke to them, saying, 'All authority has been given to Me in heaven and on earth. Go therefore … '" (Matthew 28:18–19). To this day, when the church comes together to worship Him and to hear the Word, they receive the flow of His authority and His commission to go and share Jesus with every person, transforming our world with His power.

Presenting Our Offerings

Here is man's call to open his heart and his hand. Giving in church worship is not a supportive device for God's program, as though it hung on the precarious edge of impending failure. It is as a plan that He has given to us to release us from selfishness and to allow our entry into His covenant of material blessings.

At the heart of the offering of worship is the offering of my life. When Paul wrote to the Corinthians, "He who sows sparingly will also reap sparingly, and he who sows bountifully will also reap bountifully (2 Corinthians 9:6)," he knew that it was a spiritual dynamic built into the fabric of life. When I give my offerings of worship, I am giving part of my life. It's not difficult to understand that when I give money, it's part of my life. Someone in almost every home receives money, a salary, for an investment of his or her time and talents. You give a certain amount of your life to an employer for an agreed upon wage.

I'm not saying that we are wasting our lives in exchange for money. Instead, I'm saying that we give of ourselves and receive money in return. In response, I say, "Lord, You are my life. You have made me what I am and given me the talents to do the work by which You provide for me. Because You've been so faithful to me, I offer back to You a token of what You have given me." In offering back to God what He has given us, we open ourselves to a further flow of His resources. We acknowledge that all of our life originates in Him.

Presenting your life as an offering to the Lord doesn't always involve giving money. Money isn't all we have to offer. We are to offer ourselves in living and speaking the Word of God. Giving of ourselves in service—helping people, caring, loving, and being a living example—is a part of bringing offerings to the Lord. Let's never freeload on the abundance of God's kindness to us. Let's become people who live in the wisdom of the offerings of worship—offerings out of what we have and out of what we are.

Anthropo-*what?*

God designed worship to be fulfilling to man, but there is one problem—a monstrous theological fly in this ointment of pro-spective joy: *anthropocentrism.* Anthropocentric means "centered in man." It's a term cast up by any theologian who is nervous about "experience" oriented spirituality. It's the unpardonable sin in some quarters of evangelical orthodoxy.

On the one hand, we need such warnings. We need to avoid humanistic systems that deify man and reduce God to a parlor pet, often making Him something slightly grander than trees and flowers. In that sense, anthropocentrism describes the mindset of shallow pop Christian Retail Official Sales Statistics theologies birthed in every generation. These are systems that satisfy man's desire to acknowledge God, yet still pursue his own indulgences. With respect to this use, warnings against anthropocentrism are words of wisdom—beware!

However, "man-centeredness" is also a buzzword that is often used by clerics at the hint of *anything* human; people being "blessed" or holiness becoming too "happy." There are some theological purists who feel called relentlessly to defend God's honor, even when their defense is leveled against some of His own people who not only simply love Him but who love Him simply. Thus, it seems predictable that any challenge to a proposition that worship is required by God to be "solely *unto* Him and solely *for* Him" might invite charges of man-centeredness.

However, just as the validity of the proposition "worship is for people" is shown by the natural joy its exercise generates, so the Bible demonstrates its soundness. Worship is a gift to bless rather than a chore to wearily fulfill.

A Bible-centered approach to worship clearly reveals that worship is definitely *not* a God-built device to get man to stroke a Heavenly ego. Neither is it a summons to a weekly reaffirmation of one's expertise in precision-cut declarations of doctrinal posturing. Instead, the Scriptures consistently show God calling His creatures to worship in His presence that He might release, redeem, renew, and restore them.

God respected and rewarded Abel because his worship acknowledged the one path by which man received God's loving coverage for his sin. His blood sacrifice was based on a gratitude for the redemption plan initiated in the garden, and his worship forecast an expectation of an even greater expression of love—a coming Redeemer. Cain was rejected, not so much for his violation of a religious formula as for the smallness of his jealous heart that failed to grasp the largeness of God's (2 Corinthians 9:6).

Israel was called forth from Egypt "that they may serve Me." His plan that they "serve" Him was not a relocated slavery—from Egypt's bricks to Sinai's rituals. His deliverance was out of bondage into *worship*; through worshipping Him, they would come to know the heart and nature of the One who had promised, "I will bring you up ... to a land flowing with milk and honey" (Exodus 3:17).

Into the New Testament, the concept remains constant. One of Jesus' most profound statements about worship happened during a conversation with an immoral woman filling her water jar at a well. He was clearly welcoming her away from her emptiness to be filled with the love of God who is seeking the worship of honest hearts like hers (John 4:3–26). Paul called the Romans to present themselves as people of worship. Why? So that they could come to know the goodness, the desirability, and the perfection of God's purpose in their lives (Romans 12:1–2).

The danger of falling prey to anthropocentrism melts when the Word of God is at the center of our thought process. These brief examples are sufficient to illustrate that—according to God's *heart* and Word—worship is for people.

Yet the disposition of Church history works against our pure responses to simple truth. The flow of human traditions seems to go from life to death. So often in institutions the tendency is that the practices giving rise to the life of the organization eventually degenerate into being done only for the sake of the doing. Church worship has been the victim of this human tendency. Inertia brings inevitable death. What began with vital life becomes a mere form with only an empty habit remaining.

A Central Concern: People

The class worked through their semester reports, accumulating insights and observations indicating that churches, pastors, buildings, choirs, and even liturgies were seldom the *cause* of ineffectiveness. A lost consciousness *of people* was as much at fault as any lost consciousness of God.

Wherever vital spiritual life was found in a congregation, their worship was serving as a *means* to *meet human need*. This may have not been the studied perspective in any of those churches, but it did characterize their meetings' results—they were meeting people's needs. No one seemed to be "using worship" as a self-serving tool, and the pristine vision of worship-unto-the-Lord was *not* being corrupted. Services weren't manipulated to serve human whims, nor was God being expected to jump through a hoop to meet human demands.

I learned a lot with that class. I learned that our fellowship with God in worship was two-way. God desires to meet our needs and fulfill us as much as He desires our expressions of praise and thanksgiving.

Because of what I learned in that class, my perspective on the *reason* for worship changed without sacrificing my essential Bible-centeredness or my God-centeredness.

However, I was clear on this now—with God, *we're* at the center of His concern, even when we worship.

I didn't know how much more there was to learn about it, but I liked the idea of leading people to worship. I liked it more than I ever had before, because I knew I was preparing something "in His presence" that would mean "fullness of joy." It wasn't long until I was able to apply these discoveries. They established the initial emphasis in the small pastorate to which I was soon to be called.

4

The Key to New Life

"I wish you'd oil that lock," I said;
"I've had a nasty time getting the key to turn!"
The Proprietor looked at my key, smiled, took it and gave
me another. "I should think it will be much easier now
that you have the right one."

ANNA AND I, along with our four children, accepted the little congregation in Van Nuys about a year later. There were eighteen members. We were there on a temporary assignment while I was still teaching at the Bible College. Although our term of service there was uncertain, I was anxious to try what the Holy Spirit had been making vibrant within me. I was ready to pastor with this proposition governing my approach to services and other gatherings: *worship is an opportunity for man to invite God's power and presence to move among those worshipping Him.*

Along with that truth, I had begun to see yet another concept—since worship is *for* people, it could also be the key to evangelism. It followed that if God "moves in"—if He truly wants to be present in power and bless His people at worship services—then people would be drawn to Christ. Would previously unyielded hearts sense the reality of His presence and open to Him?

The laboratory of pastoral experience has verified that they do indeed![1]

We have found that worship is the *pathway* and the *atmosphere* for people—the saved and the unsaved alike—to discover their:

- royal calling in Christ
- high destiny in life
- fullest personal worth
- deepest human fulfillment

Here again, tradition must be confronted, questioned, and adjusted if we are to realize God's maximum benefits during worship. I had been ignorant of worship as a means by which we could realize God's presence consistently. I had grown to depend on preaching alone as the instrument bringing people to repentance. Suddenly I was finding a teamwork between the Spirit and the Word—the Holy Spirit softening hearts as we worshipped and the Word enlightening people's eyes in that new atmosphere of love. This also changed the nature of my appeal. Invitations, which, early in my ministry, had been wrestling matches of the will, were now simpler and approached with a different mind-set.

I became convinced that God's program of redemption *does not* require of any man a ritual denouncing his humanness, though it *does* require a renouncing of his sin. Biblical repentance does not require submission to a predigested, dictated, dehumanizing recitative that blasts the sinner for his sinfulness, but it does require a full-hearted turning from one's own way to Jesus Christ—to acknowledge ourselves as lost and Him as the only Savior, to acknowledge ourselves as dead in sin and Him as Resurrected Lord. The spirit of worship made sure our evangelistic approach was not a humanistic program of self-ascent, while at the same time preempting a theological program of self-debasement.

When worship is warm, it provides the ideal setting for evangelistic results. Where "worship is for people," man's highest possibilities are affirmed—*truly* affirmed as a people come before the Throne of their Creator.

It is there we *find Him* who created us for joy.

It is there we *find redemption* from all that would destroy or diminish our joy. Such an approach in worship becomes an honest and humble, yet a joyous and hopeful, acknowledgment of:

1. God's great *love* for us, verified in His Son Jesus (Ephesians 2:4–5)
2. God's great *forgiveness*, insuring acceptance before him (Ephesians 1:3–6)
3. God's great *purpose* in us, establishing worth and dignity (Ephesians 2:6–10)
4. God's great *promises* to us, giving confidence for tomorrow (2 Peter 1:4)

Small wonder thousands of souls have opened their lives to Jesus in this atmosphere!

And Then, Growth

As the small pastorate began to grow, we established the workability of the transformed viewpoint that I had gained with my students. Permanent, enduring verification accrued to establish the threefold proposition:

1. Worship is for people
    2. Worship welcomes Kingdom power
    3. Worship is the key to evangelism

As I led my people in worship—with a commitment to glorify God, but with an equal pledge to believe He wanted to save, satisfy, and dignify man—true personal fulfillment blossomed in an ever-growing number of people. Moreover, the Holy Spirit began knitting us into a marvelously loving fellowship. For where God's love is responded to, a love for one another overflows. We would sing:

> Come, O Lord, and overflow us with Your love,
> Come, O Lord, and overflow us with Your love,
> For we lift our hearts like vessels
> To the everflowing stream,
> Come, O Lord, and overflow us with Your love.[2]

And He would do it!

As He did, I was amazed at the remarkable harvest of souls. People were being saved, and the incredible thing to me—having been raised on the notion that evangelistic sermons are essential to evangelistic results—was that *worship* was the source of this mighty moving of the Holy Spirit among us. People were receiving Jesus Christ, not because I "preached them under conviction," but because they sensed the presence of God as we worshipped His Majesty. The Word of Truth I taught became *life* in that atmosphere of praise, and that *life* was begotten in the hearers as the warmth of God's presence invaded our worship.

I am totally persuaded that worship is the key to evangelism as well as to the edification of the Church. Amid childlike, full-hearted worship, God's love distills like refreshing dew upon us. As worship moves beyond a merely objective exercise demanded by theological posturing, and as it becomes a simple, subjective quest for God, He responds. He answers the hunger of earnest hearts and reveals Himself in personal, transforming, and fulfilling ways. The hungry and thirsty are filled as we seek Him in our worship. In His loving mercy, He delights to come into our midst, to ignite His Word, pour out His Spirit, breathe His life, and touch with His hand of power.

Who's Invited?

Who do *you* want to come to church and who does *God* want there? How you answer this question will determine everything about how you worship God when people gather with you. If worship is only the privileged right of an approved membership, schooled in the acceptable forms of the given group, the outsider may be allowed to attend, but he will essentially remain "outside." The idea that "everyone is welcome" doesn't stick if there is no welcoming atmosphere—even if unintentionally. However, when we lead worship in such a way as to be accessible to all, in an atmosphere of hope and joy, then church services become an open doorway, not a guarded fortress.

I submit that God never intended worship to be an occasion for proving one's expertise in religion, but for satisfying one's hunger and thirst for God.

I believe that God meant Sunday morning not to become a weekly test of personal orthodoxy, but to provide the opening of a reservoir of refreshing by inspiration, insight and blessing.

I contend that, as long as treat worship as a way to protect God from unworthy participants, it can never serve His purpose as a resource for incomplete and broken mankind to find completion and wholeness in His presence.

I also believe that *worship is for people,* not the other way around. God does not first *receive* worship. He first *gives* it. Just as God gave the Sabbath to allow rest for His most noble creature, God has given worship as a means for man's:

- Recovery
- Restoration
- Reviving
- Redemption
- Refreshing

Yet, as the Pharisees had turned the Sabbath into an impossible system of ritual observance, prohibiting a joyous participation by the average person, some have elevated the idea of worship to a place that few can attain because of the insistent demands of ritual performance or theological expertise.

Sequence is the issue. God's *gift is first.* God has given worship to everyone as a privileged resource, not as a private regimen for His scrutiny. The gathering of people in His Name should be an occasion when hungry and searching souls find an atmosphere of warmth and acceptance.

I've decided to risk the protest of the spiritual purist: "Humanistic! Idolatrous! Anthropocentric! Vanity of vanities!" However, before flashing red lights explode in the halls of ecclesiastical orthodoxy, let no one mistake me:

> In saying that worship is *for* man, I haven't said worship is *to* him. Moreover, in saying worship is a gift to man, I didn't say it is not to be expressed *unto* God.

He—the Transcendent and Eternal One—is still the Person in our worship. However, in approaching the task of leading worship, as I have declared it here, each time I step before my flock, I sense God's pleasure. I am leading them to Him, but I am doing it by means of a *gift* He has given for their blessing. Worship is for *them* and I learned that they experience growth in every way as they receive this gift of worship as something that is *theirs*.

I think you'll find the same, for thousands who joined with me in this discovery have come to attest to the vitality of these facts:

1. God has provided worship as a means of entry to our rejoicing in the presence of the Ultimate Reality.
2. Worship introduces dimensions of possibility in every life that transcend our sin and our self-imposed limitations as we welcome the Transcendent One.
3. Worshipping God brings the highest sense of dignity humanity we can know, for the regal nature of His Majesty begins to flow downward and inward.

The greatest issue we face is not so much that we immediately perceive the depth of our sin and weakness or even the greatness of God's grace and power. The primary issue is whether we will come—will we be *led* before His Throne and *seek Him*. Because if we do, heaven will break loose *on earth!*

In our church, the passage of nearly two decades has seen tremendous growth in people, an increase in attendance to nearly 10,000 each week,[3] and a garnering of nearly 30,000 decisions for Christ during that time—all flowing from this mindset concerning worship's priority and its purpose.

In addition, during those years, time and again in my study of the Scriptures, the Holy Spirit has unveiled notable personalities of the Bible as case studies in the power and purpose of worship. I'd like to share some of those "unveilings" with you in the following chapters.

5

Fumbling Forward in Faith

"The simple beauty in the first tottering steps of a child, overshadowing all absence of grace and form, is seeing the sheer sparkle of joy's adventure in his eyes. The progress is so small but the accomplishment so great."

ABRAHAM IS A paradox in terms.

He is honored in the gallery of the faithful, but he lied about his relationship with his wife, virtually surrendering her body to the whim of a pagan king. He is called the father of faith, but in an effort to beget a promised child, he fathered a problem child. The diplomacy of world governments is tested to this day as a result. How does it happen that so human, fallible, and fear-filled a person can gain a reputation for "faith"?

While watching a televangelist preaching on "Boldness and Authority with God," I was somewhat taken aback by his zealous effort on the subject. Of course, I appreciated his intent and I wouldn't criticize his spirit, but I was troubled at his approach.

"I want you to look at Abraham," he exhorted. "Here is a man of faith—the 'father of our faith,' the Bible says. I want you to see the authority of faith that he shows. He gained such a place in God that he entered into consultation with Him as to what God was going to do in great cities. He boldly called on God to rescue Sodom and Gomorrah. Imagine it, saints! One man moving God's hand of action. That is faith. That is boldness. That is authority with God. That's what I'm talking about."

Now, some people might be irritated with every aspect of this preacher's words. The whole idea of such intimacy with and rulership under God is foreign to the perception of many earnest believers. However, that isn't what bothered me. I do believe there is a grand arena of possibility for our intercession with God, one that fulfills His higher intentions for us as His sons and daughters. Rather, what disturbed me was the unwitting, but real, dishonesty of the proposition as he presented it. Besides hinting that Abraham's interaction with God was like that of a brash kid issuing demands to his father, the whole episode was removed from the human context in which the Bible casts this remarkable man. However bold his intercession may have been, the whole story not only depicts Abraham's approach as humbly hesitant, but the next chapter recites another instance of his fumbling humanity.

The same man who the Bible describes in Genesis 19 as making a bold appeal for the sparing of cities, will, in the next chapter, trade his integrity and his wife's chastity to save his own neck. It's hardly a picture of an accomplished master of faith! I strongly resist such projections of "the faith life" as the televangelist made, not because I would discourage a bold, believing lifestyle, but because the Bible doesn't describe such a life as superhuman. There is nothing more self-defeating in the communication of God's call to supernatural living than suggesting a grandiose or contrived, affected piety that is outside the scope of what the Bible actually describes. I like the proposition inherent in the book title, *Extraordinary Living for Ordinary Men*, (an old book by Sam Shoemaker). God's power in human flesh will hopefully make us less "carnal," but it will never make us less human!

A close examination of Abraham's life does provide great lessons in faith's growth, and the New Testament does hold him forth as faith's "father"—one in whose steps we are to walk (Romans 4:11–12).

However, this assessment of his life is made after the fact—after a lifetime of growth, and after the final evaluation of a man's life made following his very human earthly sojourn. Abraham was called. He answered. He learned at times and was blindly doltish at others. He succeeded on some occasions and failed on others—always moving forward in faith, but often fumbling as he groped his way ahead.

This isn't to demean Abraham or disrespect the marvelous witness he left to us. God's Word endorses his life with these words: he "obtained a good testimony through faith" (Hebrews 11:39). I'm not suggesting anything less, but I don't believe the testimony of the faithful is there to intimidate us. Their stories are in the Bible to build our belief so that we can do the same!

In Abraham's case, the hallmark of a holy habit merits our study—a look into a continuing trait of his that brought about his accomplishments in "faith." What stands out is this: whether stumbling, succeeding, fumbling, or failing, the one outstanding, discernible feature of his character is that he lived his life before the altar of God.

In the short dozen pages the Bible takes to tell the whole story of Abraham, there are nearly a dozen times we see him worshipping at an altar. His worship-walk points the path to understanding how today's believer may advance in God's will.

It isn't surprising to find in Abraham's life the same issues that God began to remedy in Adam's, a restoration of fellowship and fruitfulness—of relationship and rulership.

In Paul's classic elaboration of justification by faith, Abraham is a case study of the gargantuan truth that faith, not works, establishes an individual's relationship with God. In this context (which embraces us as those redeemed unto the same status of divine acceptance), the Bible describes Abraham as one who received "the promise that he would be heir of the world." With this, direct mention is made that this same promise was to be "to his seed" (Romans 4:13). These are prophetic words speaking to us—to today's believer. To be a "world-heir" doesn't require the ability to control Wall Street or to succeed in Hollywood, but it does mean we can overcome the ruling spirit of this world. We can "reign in life" by the power of Jesus Christ's life within us. Thus, Abraham's pilgrimage isn't just a historical study. It's a model for our possibilities too!

The summary Paul makes of Abraham's life speaks of restored dominion, of recovered rulership. It not only applies those prospects to us, but also commands us to learn the way to the same by walking "in the steps of the faith which our father Abraham *had*" (Romans 4:12). Upon examination, we find those steps constantly leading to an altar of worship, with each experience teaching us how even the human and the fumbling may find their inheritance as "heirs of the world."

The opening pages of Genesis unfold Abraham's altar experiences like a chain reaction of growth in faith, revealing a worshipping believer who moved forward in possessing God's purpose for him. Though human fallibility brings periodic fumbling, his call as a world-heir is ultimately unimpeded by that humanness as his experiences at God's altar progressively transform him—effecting "altar-actions," we might say. Abraham is proof that fumbling saints can find their way forward as humanness and holiness converge in the fragility of human flesh. There are several altars in Abraham's experience. His worship-walk offers lessons for our own steps of progress—from our *calling* to a life of faith to our eventual *overcoming* as victors in faith. Let's look at the principles of how worship moves us forward in faith.

The First Altar: Accepting God's Promises

> Then the Lord appeared to Abram and said, "To your descendants I will give this land." And there he built an altar to the Lord, who had appeared to him (Genesis 12:7).

There is an abiding reluctance in every thoughtful person that shies away from promises of personal significance. Only the gullible leap at proposals of impending greatness awaiting them. Only the naive believe without hesitation. I have met hundreds of people who have supposed that because they at first doubt such God-given promises, they will never be qualified for "faith." However, the definition of faith is not wide-eyed gullibility, nor does it require an instant "go-for-it" action. The first point of faith is simply to be open to God's promise, even when it seems beyond our ability to contain it. There is a better way to respond to God's higher promises than to remain hesitant. We must take the promise; receive it, but take it to the altar of worship.

Abraham wasn't having delusions of grandeur. God was speaking to him. Neither is it an illusion that God still speaks to people and confirms to their hearts that His Word holds high promise for their own life situations in the here-and-now.

There's no way we can replay Abraham's thoughts to know how closely they parallel our own when grand promise awakens hope in our souls. However, we could presume that God's Word shocked Abraham. Although the Bible says, "He did not waver at the promise of God through unbelief, but was strengthened in faith, giving glory to God" (Romans 4:20), it doesn't say he wasn't surprised. God's call to faith may stun us but it need not stagger us. Abraham was steadfast, not because he was less vulnerable to doubt than the rest of us; he stood firm because he went to his knees at an altar, "giving glory to God."

This is the first principle of advancing in faith: worshipping the Giver of the promise reminds us of His power to perform and His faithfulness to keep it.

The Second Altar:
Learning More of the Promiser

> And he moved from there to the mountain east of Bethel, and ... there he built an altar to the Lord and called on the name of the Lord. So Abram journeyed, going on still toward the South (Genesis 12:8–9).

There is more than a continuing practice of altar-building and worshipping indicated here, for the statement that Abraham "called on the name of the Lord" points to a growing knowledge of God. The "name" of the Lord reflects His nature, His Person and His character. Abraham was journeying onward, but his travels do more than acquaint him with the tough issues of life. He is also learning the trustworthy nature of his Lord.

I was recently contacted by an irate person who flared his temper at me, attacking the ministry of the church I pastor based on one issue: "A member of your pastoral staff said …" and the person went on to say what he had said and done.

I was appalled.

It wasn't a charge of immorality, financial dishonesty, or doctrinal error. The charge was of gross insensitivity toward a person who had called for help. In responding, I didn't retaliate or deny the charge. I simply asked how the caller knew all that had been said. Although I didn't say it to the caller, I knew what had been said wasn't true. I knew it—not because I was there, not because I presumed perfection among our staff, and not because I was defensive—but because I knew the man who was being accused. I knew he was incapable of acting the way that had been described. (Indeed, when the whole matter was resolved, what actually had happened was not even remotely related to the purported "facts" that had been hurled at me over the telephone.)

Every one of us faces a parallel reality regularly. It's the reality that a liar, the Arch-Deceiver, is ever-present to contest the trustworthiness of God—especially when time passes and promises we have received from Him haven't yet been fulfilled. Trying circumstances sometimes force questions about the strength of our faith and the certainty of His faithfulness. The Accuser will charge God—bombarding one's mind with incriminating remarks and seeking to remove our sense of security in the Father's Word.

When he attacks God's nature or assails one's sense of confidence, ongoing and sustained worship is the key to conquest. When I walk each day into His presence, worshipping Him, and allowing the Holy Spirit to make Jesus' "name"—His faithfulness, His healing, His loving, His keeping power—real to me, I'll keep steadfast. Learning to know more of the Promiser keeps me strong in trusting His promises, even when hope is attacked and self-doubts seek to dominate me.

The Third Altar: Returning to the Start

Then Abram went up from Egypt ... to the place
of the altar which he had made there at first
(Genesis 13:1–4).

From the place of his second altar, Abraham seemed to make a
detour. His trip to Egypt appeared to be (1) undirected by God,
(2) characterized by compromise, yet (3) climaxed by prosperity
(Genesis 12:10–20). However, with the climax came an expul-
sion: "They sent him away" (Genesis 12:20).

We could wish for a detailed report filling in the months of
Abraham's presumptuous descent into Egypt. The motive is
given—there was famine and he sought food—but his method
was the pursuit of personal supply in his own wisdom. The
resultant compromising of his integrity, involving the exploita-
tion of his wife's beauty, would have brought further failure
had not God intervened. However, the interposing sovereign
grace drew Abraham back to Bethel and back to worship. God's
faithful protection graciously restored whatever may have
been ignorantly lost through his fleshly efforts at self-provision.
Abraham worshipped God, having returned to the place of his
beginning.

He is not alone in having drifted from God's best through
humanly motivated enterprise. However sincere we may have
been at certain times, all of us have stepped outside the will of
God in well-intended quests at solving our own problems. The
beauty of studying this event in the life of faith's father is that
it holds hope for me. The same God who laid hold of Abraham
when faith faltered and blindly sought its own way is the One
who today will bring back anyone who will allow it. In so many

games we learned in our childhood, returning to "Start" meant to lose everything one had gained to that point. There are many stumbling believers who feel the same way about God, as though His displeasure with their failures means they face a life of interminable frustration. However, where God can find a worshipper whose heart is bent beside his knee at an altar of praise to Him for His mercy and grace, there is a marvelously wonderful promise: "Let the lawless forsake his way and the unrighteous man his scheming. Let him return to the Lord, and He will have mercy on him; and to our God, for He will abundantly pardon" (Isaiah 55:7 author's paraphrase).

Abundant pardon! There is no wealth like this reward.

There may be no way to forget the foolishness of our blind pursuits that end in cul-de-sacs, but the God we began with in worship will seek us there, and draw us back to the beginning.

When He does, worship Him at once. He doesn't require a waiting period for the returnees—a proving time before receiving worship. He welcomes your worship and your return to fullness just as surely as He did before.

The Fourth Altar: Enlarging Your Horizons of Hope

> And the Lord said to Abram ... "Lift your eyes now and look ... all the land which you see I give to you" ... Then Abram moved *his* tent ... and built an altar there to the Lord (Genesis 13:14–18).

The most noteworthy trait of Abraham's worship-walk was that it was always a response. God dealt with him and Abraham worshipped.

There is an unspoken wisdom here that we might overlook unless it's underlined: worship transcends our weakness while acknowledging God's power.

Reestablished in the land, the Lord later challenged Abraham again. God had earlier promised "this land," but now He began to specify dimensions: "northward, southward, eastward and westward … Arise, walk in the land through its length and its width for I give it to you" (Genesis 13:14–17). What was a general statement that allowed for Abraham's interpretation was now quite specific, and the boundaries must have been much grander than Abraham had earlier imagined.

Abraham's story is one of the believing life.

Whatever joy, blessing, and fulfillment any of us has discovered in our early walk with Christ, inevitably we come to a place of confrontation with God. He who will never allow us to stagnate, or to settle for the small or the shallow, ever draws us to loftier heights and deeper depths.

Have you ever experienced His deeper call to know Him better, or His higher call to serve Him at new levels? How have you felt when He calls? Weak? Insufficient? Uncertain? Hesitant?

If so, let us learn together the lesson of Abraham's fourth altar. Worship is the way to receive the promise of possibilities larger than you ever imagined. Worship is the way to respond to God when you feel you are incapable of understanding His call. Respond to Him. "Faithful is the One who calls you—He will also accomplish it!" (1 Thessalonians 5:24 author's paraphrase).

Toward "World-Heirs"

These four instances launch us in applying worship to a walk that moves toward the "world-heir" life of dominion and restored rulership that Jesus died to give us. There are two power-principles in Abraham's other experiences that drew him to the altar of worship:

1. *Genesis 14:18–20.* Abraham applies the principle of worshipful giving in response to the blessings of victory and provision. His tithe to Melchizedek acknowledges the Lord as both our Provider, and as the Possessor of all things—the One from whom we receive the privilege of anything we are given and everything we have.

2. *Genesis 15:10–21.* Abraham exercises the principle of worship as spiritual warfare. God honors his sacrifice with a great promise concerning the future of Abraham's offspring. The effort of vultures to seize the sacrifice so worshipfully offered, and Abraham's rising to drive them away, is a potent picture of the believer's contending in worship against the hosts of hell who seek to overthrow God's purposes for us, our children, and our household.

Along with these, a series of three events in succeeding chapters powerfully demonstrates the developments that we can expect to flow from a maturing worshipper's life. Each event is a worship experience because, in each, we learn a new submission to God's purpose and exercise a new power in God's kingdom.

1. *Chapter 17: The exercise of life-begetting power.* God calls Abraham to accept the sign of circumcision as a token of the covenant between God and him. He does so at the price of blood, pain, and the acceptance of a world that mocked the practice—thereby presenting his body as a living sacrifice unto God (Romans 12:1–2), and thereby

paving the way to Isaac's birth and the fulfillment of God's promise.

2. *Chapter 18: The exercise of intercessory power.* God relates to Abraham the impending doom of Sodom and Gomorrah, entrusting to this man of covenant the possibility of beginning to learn the ruling faith inherent in intercession. Abraham's humility and boldness mix, and the God he worships unveils His heart of mercy and effects a divine rescue of the few redeemable inhabitants of a reprobate culture.

3. *Chapter 20: The exercise of healing power.* God answers Abraham's intercessory prayer for the healing of the women of Abimelech's household—a notable example of Abraham as a fumbler-forward-in-faith. On the heels of his reverting to earlier fear and compromise, repentance brings a release of great faith and power. The reversal of his confusion opens the door to his ministering a reversal of his sin's consequences.

This progression of a man moving from his first steps in faith to his perception of himself as an intercessor for nations and a minister of God's healing power is indicative of the fruit of worship. This is not an accidental byproduct but a process originating from the divine intent of God. Our focus on worship as the God-given means to return man to rule is simply and practically manifest in faith's father, Abraham, whom every New Testament believer should emulate.

Worship's Highest Dominion—Surrender

Nevertheless, we cannot completely understand the glory of such a way of victory and dominion until we come to Abraham's final lesson in worship. It is here that our greatest understanding of ruling and reigning with Christ occurs—when we come to learn that the highest dominion is gained through our surrender of everything we hold dear. God tested Abraham, saying, "Take now your son, your only *son* Isaac, whom you love, and go to the land of Moriah, and offer him there as a burnt offering on one of the mountains of which I shall tell you" (Genesis 22:2).

The Lord called Abraham to sacrifice his son. That sounds hideous, doesn't it? In fact, it seemed a perversion of God's nature as Abraham understood it and as God's nature truly is. *"What happened to this God that I serve?"* Abraham must have thought. Nevertheless, Abraham followed the Lord, notwithstanding what seemed to be a frightening, tormenting vision of his only son slain on a pile of wood and going up in flames.

Abraham's answer to the call to worship brought him to a place called Moriah, where God directed that he go and offer the sacrifice.

> Then they came to the place of which God had told him. And Abraham built an altar there and placed the wood in order; and he bound Isaac his son and laid him on the altar, upon the wood. And Abraham stretched out his hand and took the knife to slay his son.
>
> But the Angel of the Lord called to him from heaven and said, "Abraham, Abraham!"
>
> So he said, "Here I am."
>
> And He said, "Do not lay your hand on the lad, or do anything to him; for now I know that you fear God, since you have not withheld your son, your only *son*, from Me" (Genesis 22:9–12).

The Bible tells us that the Lord provided another sacrifice. Abraham turned and saw a ram caught by his horns in a thicket, and he offered the ram in place of Isaac. The Bible tells us one more thing. It tells us in Hebrews 11:17–19 that Abraham was so certain of the faithful nature of God that he believed that if he *did* slay Isaac, God would raise him from the dead.

Genesis 22 is a love story and a case of a world-heir entering into his largest inheritance:

1. It reveals God's love for Abraham, in inviting him to enter the fellowship of the Father, as one who loves and trusts enough to sacrifice His Son.
2. It reveals Abraham's love for God, refusing to doubt God even when it appeared that God was about to violate His own nature in requiring human sacrifice.
3. It reveals Isaac's love for Abraham, by his submission and trust that his father would only obey God if it was in the best interest of everyone—including Isaac.

Here is true dominion.

This is worship rising beyond mere power into the fullest dimensions of partnership with God—into "the fellowship of His sufferings, being conformed to His death" (Philippians 3:10). The worshipper may learn to surmount life's obstacles, overcome his own fumbling humanity, and move into the exercise of power with God, but never let the quest for "ruling with Christ" be separated from worship that learns of "dying with Christ." They must be knit together and kept in a balanced perspective, because our "ruling with Christ" always flows from a partnership of "dying with Christ."

You need not be a religious expert or mystical saint to rise to such height. A very human "forward-fumbler" can qualify—if he keeps worshipping.

6

Unshackling Your Future

"Thine eye diffused a quick'ning ray, I woke,
the dungeon flamed with light.
My chains fell off; my heart was free,
I rose, went forth and followed Thee."
Charles Wesley

Non sequitur: "I always thought you had pretty eyes, but isn't the soccer team going to play tomorrow?"

Non sequitur: "Ken called and said the weather man predicted rain today. I really loved playing marbles when we lived on Lexington Street."

Non sequitur: "What would you rather? Or go fishing?"

Non sequiturs.

They are those abrupt, illogical turns of thought and speech that have no apparent relationship to one another—remarks that have no bearing on what came before. Because *non sequiturs* are usually indicative of the scatterbrained or the irrational, we don't find them in the Bible. However, there is a place where one seems to occur. In the middle of a conversation between God and Moses, an exchange takes place that defies logic—unless we are ready to change our thinking about worship.

The setting: Mount Sinai—also called Horeb—the Mountain of God.

The occasion: The commissioning of Moses at the burning bush to go into Egypt and command Pharaoh to release the Israelite slaves.

Moses asks, "Who *am* I that I should go to Pharaoh, and that I should bring the children of Israel out of Egypt?" The Lord answers, "I will certainly be with you. And this *shall* be a sign to you that I have sent you: When you have brought the people out of Egypt, you shall serve [worship] God on this mountain" (Exodus 3:11–12).

Read it again ... and listen.

Question: "Who am I to attempt so great a program of deliverance?"

Answer: "I'll be with you. You bring the people here to worship Me."

Non sequitur? It seems like one, doesn't it? Moses' question has to do with his qualifications, but God's answer has to do with the issue of worship. The exchange between the Lord and Moses isn't illogical, but the power in the logic and the lesson it contains cannot be firmly grasped without our confronting a common problem of perspective. We all tend to lack the essential viewpoint. Our usual approach to the Book of Exodus demonstrates the need.

The Trouble with the Ten Commandments

To the contemporary believer *The Ten Commandments* are not only the Decalogue tablets of stone, but also the title of a motion picture. It is a problem that probably more people envision the Exodus as portrayed by Cecil B. DeMille than as reported by Moses, the Prophet of God. The story's drama is a setup for Hollywood's special effects to attempt recreating the phenomenal and the miraculous—plenty of grist for the screenwriter's mill. However, Exodus ends in the movie version as only the story of Israel's deliverance. It's more than that: Exodus is a book about the power and purpose of worship.

The real issue of Exodus jarred me when I saw the apparent *non sequitur*. As a bewildered Moses expresses doubt about his own qualifications, God says, "Bring the people to this mountain." My first reaction was, "God wasn't listening to Moses." However, when I prayed through the text, something clicked and my perspective became clear. Those words brought me to an awareness of the hidden secret of God's purpose for Israel and His key to their destiny. The pathway to His purpose was the pathway to worship. The way of deliverance—of unshackling their future—was not so much an open sea as an awaiting mountain. There they would hear from God and come to know Him as they worshipped Him according to His will and His way.

Let's take a fresh look at Exodus from this viewpoint.

The Real Issue in Exodus

"The most dramatic coming-of-age party in history" may seem an irreverent description of Israel's deliverance under Moses' leadership, but it's certainly an apt one. Just as a young woman of wealthy parentage enters the social scene with a splash of splendor, God shook the status quo of the ancient world and made a statement about His power and His people. He not only drained the resources of the richest monarchy of the time, bringing Egypt to its knees, but the display of His miraculous power had such an impact on the news media of the time that four decades later nations still trembled at the memory of His workings (Joshua 2:10). As thrilling and as electrifying as the flow of events is in the first half of Exodus, the sensation turns our attention from the real issue.

Exodus is primarily a study in the power of worship to release people, but it's hard to secure that focus with a Heston-like figure looming above you. Our vision of worship blurs before the onset of overpowering scenes as a towering figure stretches his rod over the storm-tossed sea, miraculously splitting it apart. Alternatively, we envision the same figure coming down the side of Sinai like a giant with a glowing face, gripping stone tablets under one muscular arm, their engraving still steaming from the touch of God's finger. The overwhelming explosiveness of the plagues and the powerful works of God render it somewhat difficult to see worship at the center of Exodus: but it is.

In the book of Exodus, worship is the *heart*, the *core*, the *issue*, the *key*, the *destiny*, the *center*, and *above* all else. Consider:

1. *Worship is at the heart* of Moses' commission: "Bring the people here that they may worship me" (Exodus 3:12 author's paraphrase). Their release is to allow their worship; God's promise is to meet them when they do. He is not only calling them to liberty; He is calling them to intimacy. He is sending a deliverer not only to free them, but also to bring them to Himself. Since God enunciates His desire so clearly—to liberate His people that they might come to know His love—it is clear that worship is at the heart.

2. *Worship is at the core* of the message the Lord told Moses to give to Pharaoh: "and you shall say to him, 'The Lord God of the Hebrews has met with us; and now, please, let us go three days' journey into the wilderness that we may sacrifice to the Lord our God.'" (Exodus 3:18). Pharaoh rejected that request not only because he wanted to retain the convenience of slaves, but also because he knew that a

people free to worship God can never be bound by earthly powers. Because the spirit of the world will always seek to retain oppressive power over God's own, worship is at the core of God's message.

3. *Worship is at issue* in the power struggle between Pharaoh and God. The monarch's willful resistance to the Almighty's declared purpose rested on his own refusal to honor God: "Who is the Lord that I should do this?" (Exodus 5:2 author's paraphrase). But God would have exalted Pharaoh as well as delivered Israel had he listened and obeyed: "for this *purpose* I have raised you up, that I may show My power *in* you, and that My Name may be declared in all the earth" (Exodus 9:16). Pharaoh had the opportunity to become a worshipper of the Lord God, and had he done so he might have become known forever as the greatest emancipator in history. Instead, he chose to resist God and became a study in hardness of heart and the leader in one of history's most devastating defeats. In determining whether God's declaration would bring him blessing or judgment, the question will be resolved by his releasing of a people to worship their God (and whether he will acknowledge God as greater than himself). Worship is at issue.

4. *Worship is the key* to Israel's protection from the final plague as well as to the practical provision of nourishment for the first stage of their journey ahead. The sacrifice of the Passover Lamb renews the ancient blood covenant in force since Adam. Israel's enslavement had doubtlessly reduced the frequency or removed the practice of sacrifice completely. Many had also adapted to the Egyptian systems of worship, but now the blood on their doorways will subject them to mockery. However, it also declares

their faith and ensures their deliverance. Worship is
the key.

5. *Worship is the destiny* of this people, for following upon
their arrival at Sinai, the Lord says, "You have seen what I
did to the Egyptians, and *how* I bore you on eagles' wings
and brought you to Myself. Now therefore, if you will
indeed obey My voice and keep My covenant, then you
shall be a special treasure to Me above all people; for all
the earth *is* Mine. And you shall be to Me a kingdom of
priests and a holy nation" (Exodus 19:4–6). God's objective in liberating them, vanquishing the Egyptians, and
bringing them to Sinai, is to establish a special relationship: "I brought you unto Myself. You shall be a special
treasure to Me." This covenant relationship will reveal a
national destiny—a priestly ministry to the world. Here
is to rise a "kingdom of priests"—the one people on the
earth who will not only worship God for themselves, but
who will serve as priests to lead others to do the same.
Worship is their destiny.

6. *Worship is at the center* of their lives. They use the
many months at Sinai to build a magnificent mobile
worship center: the Tabernacle. It is not a great hall for
the assembling of multitudes, but a place of personal
encounter where worshippers may bring their covenant
offerings. "And let them make Me a sanctuary [a sacred
place], that I may dwell among them … And there I
will meet with you, and I will speak with you" (Exodus
25:8,22). The arrangement of their tribes located three
clans each to the north, east, south and west, with the
Tabernacle in the middle of them all. God Himself
directed their tribal arrangement so that worship was at
the center.

7. *Worship is over and above all* in the calendar the Lord outlined for the newly enfranchised society of former slaves. It was built upon weekly Sabbaths of worship, monthly new moons of worship, and seasonal feasts of celebrative worship. With this, the year is twice highlighted by special "beginnings"—the Passover to commemorate their deliverance and the Day of Atonement to sustain their attention to holiness of heart and life. Further, the invitation of their offerings of gold, silver, jewels, and other precious objects for the building of the Tabernacle, along with their offerings of meal, oil, and animals, all form an essential part of their redeeming fellowship with God. There is no part of their life unaffected by worship, and when the Tabernacle was set in place, God crowned it all. The glory of the Lord filled the Tabernacle, and as they would travel, the cloud of God rose above, both for their direction and their protection. Worship was over and above all.

Reforming Our Perspective

My personal confrontation with the real issue in Exodus led to the above conclusions. Certainly, worship was at the heart of the book; however, what was I to do about it now? I could see that what I viewed as a *non sequitur* was the result of my orientation to think of "serving God" as something I did rather than something I was to be—that working was service rather than worshipping. A fresh analysis of Exodus had outlined the relationship between deliverance and worship—the second being the key to the first. Seeing that, God's purpose with His redeemed people became clearer: "And you shall be to Me a kingdom of priests and a holy nation ..." (Exodus 19:6).

God had intended Israel to become a kingdom of priests. His original plan was that they become a nation of spiritual leaders helping the peoples of the world to worship God. The substance and style of their worship were intended to show all mankind the way to God, and thereby worship was the way to fulfill their mission of evangelizing. This never came to fruition.

The incident of the Golden Calf dissolved it. The breakdown occurred at the foot of the same mountain where He'd called them to learn their lesson. The goal had been a whole nation serving as a priesthood to the nations. Now, with sin seeping in at the edges, Moses calls out for repentance. The plan could have been reinstated, but sadly and significantly, only one tribe answers the call, "Who is on the Lord's side?" (Exodus 32:26). Because of Levi's response, the Levites alone became the priestly tribe. The sad result is that a whole nation, intended for a globe-serving priesthood, becomes a sinning nation, barely sustaining its own spiritual life. A self-serving cycle is set in motion. They end up merely managing their own worship instead of leading the world to the worship of the Creator.

Worship was the means of their deliverance.

Worship was to be their realized destiny—the key to unchaining their future.

However, the glory that might have been, never was. It would have to wait for another era of people who would learn from their lessons and unleash the highest purposes of God.

The New Priesthood

The New Testament seems to churn with statements about a people who have failed to realize their destiny. Jesus describes God's continued search for a people who will worship Him "in spirit and in truth" (John 4:24). Repeatedly Paul declares that a new age awaits the Church—an unfolding secret of divine destiny, confounding hell and populating heaven. The promises indicate a people whose worship invites the Kingdom of God in a present visitation of power, and whose ministry declares the Kingdom of God as an eternal hope.

Two verses seem to embrace the whole of that prospect:

> Now all these things happened to them as examples, and they were written for our admonition, upon whom the ends of the ages have come (1 Corinthians 10:11).

> And all these, having obtained a good testimony through faith, did not receive the promise, God having provided something better for us, that they should not be made perfect apart from us (Hebrews 11:39–40).

The first directs us to learn from Israel's wilderness errors. The second reminds us that the new covenant holds forth possibilities in the Holy Spirit not present under the old. The first text shouts, "Don't fall prey to the lust and confusion that ruins the priestly role of the whole people." The second says, "Welcome the Holy Spirit's indwelling and overflowing, to energize your life and expand your worship." With those directives in mind, today's Church could begin something reformational. We could begin to revive the destiny God intended for His delivered people long ago. Its fulfillment hinges upon our willingness to let a reformation in worship transform our thinking and lifestyle.

The Weakness of Worship

This reformation began for me when I started to see worship differently. I had to acknowledge that I hadn't seen worship as central a force as it had been in the story of Exodus.

I was willing to allow worship a place.

I was willing to acknowledge its need, even its desirability.

However, at the bottom line I found I had to struggle with my convictions about the relative power of worship in terms of changing, reaching, confronting or saving the world. I now confess I had a great deal more confidence in strategies for evangelism and logic in preaching than I did in the miracle of worship. Thus, I viewed worship more as a part, rather than as the point, of the Church's being. Worship was the gentle lady we escorted on Sunday morning, but our systems were the business heavyweights we depended on to get the job done.

Let's face it. Few of us see worship as the Church's strength, and certainly not its frontline of power.

Worship will never make points in the world system. The world operates on the brawn of bucks, bodies, and bombs, but God operates on the power of praise, sacrifice, and humility of heart. He works through submitted souls, singing saints, and Spirit-filled sanctuaries.

Over the intervening years since I confronted the need to prioritize worship, I have discussed this belief with many people. I'm now of the opinion that any reticence toward a reformation in worship isn't merely because of a lack of perspective. I wonder how many of us simply fear the possibility that if we transformed our worship, God's power might actually manifest itself in a way we would be unable to control.

However, we must let go. Where once the Lord sent His deliverer to Pharaoh with the message "Let My people go," I believe today he would say to His Church, "My people, let go." We must slay any Pharaoh in our own souls, for Israel's exodus provides a model for today's Church. Worship is the key to unshackling the future. People who worship God will be delivered to realize their destiny. That path Israel walked before awaits those who will test its full potential. *Let God's people put worship at the center of their lives, and the glory of God will fill the house where they gather.* When it does, others will behold God in their midst and will be drawn to Him.

We must break free of the notion that today's "Exodus people"—the Church—can become truly powerful by physical strength or human wisdom. Moses' murder of the Egyptian hastened nothing of God's deliverance. Moreover, while golden calves heed the world's tastes in worship styles, idol worship will never establish a people of priestly kingdom power.

Make no mistake, these lessons point to worship as our strength. I must reject the idea that either my strength (Moses' undue zeal) or my style (Egyptian-modeled calves) are the keys to influence and accomplishment. Worship is what unlocks the doors to the highest release of Christ's purpose among His people. Worship welcomes God's presence, and thereby reveals the Lord's glory, and "all flesh"—everyday human beings—"will see it together."

When Flesh Beholds Glory

"I walked in and the instant I stepped through the door I knew I had come home."

"I was sitting there surrounded by the singing, and when you gave the invitation I discovered I was raising my hand in response."

"I listened as the worship time continued—I knew none of the songs but I couldn't stop crying. Peace filled my soul because I knew God was in this place."

"My wife and I had come as a last-ditch effort at keeping our marriage together. We couldn't explain why, but the presence of the Lord was so strong we were changed in our attitude toward Him and toward each other."

Remarks like these fill letters to my office and comments from our congregation. They are case studies in people having their future unshackled. People simply arrived to find a worshipping church—an approach to ministry that I had always thought too weak to be workable. However, even though the "weakness" of form and style would seem deficient as a means of impressing visitors or others, the power of God infused the setting to which they had come. Human wisdom, skill, or accomplishment were not the pivotal means of securing results that unshackled people and released a whole church to become a kingdom of priests.

Could this be what God meant when He said to Moses, "I will have a people who is a nation of priests to the world"? Could these responses be the result of what God meant when He said, "Bring the people to worship me and I'll lead them to a land of fulfillment and a life of purpose"?

I think so.

Therefore, even though I thought God's answer to Moses' question was a *non sequitur*, I discovered that His answer, "Bring the people to worship Me," was the right answer, even if it defied human logic.

Worship usually does.

7

Royal Bridge Building

" … the eleventh commandment is,
'Thou shalt not sweat it!'"

THERE IS SOMETHING about the word *priest* that seems unsettling to people.

If they're materialists, *priest* seems entirely irrelevant.

If they're Protestants, *priest* seems categorically Catholic.

If they're laymen, *priest* seems "beyond me."

To Joe Anybody, the average person, the word "priest" may evoke a range of feelings from suspicion to reverence—from prejudice to respect. For others, priest may awaken memories or experiences that renew the highest esteem or the deepest frustration.

I think that totaling out the above and summarizing general social opinion, the idea of "priest," in many minds, leans to the impractical and the mystical, conjuring up notions of "otherworldliness" or virtual passivity toward everyday realities.

All that, in spite of *pontifex*.

Pontifex is the Latin word for "priest." The beauty of the word is that its derivation makes it clear that "priest" is an active idea, revealing a word of positive and powerful purpose. The real meaning lies in the original definition of *pontifex*: *bridge builder*. The etymology of the word undergirds such old English words as *pont* (a bridge), *pontage* (the toll for crossing the bridge), and our contemporary term *pontoon* (a floating bridge). I dwell on all that to establish a point: God always meant priesthood to be something practical—to help us "cross over" or to "get from here to there."

That's one of the reasons the *priesthood* was one of the fighting words of the Reformation. The Reformers recognized that the priesthood had become a barricade to God rather than a bridge—a blockage instead of a blessing. The Church's oppressive control over the laity had bred horrible confusion and bondage. The confessional was corrupted through manipulation of the masses, and sin was licensed through the sale of indulgences. The trumpet call to rally every believer to the awareness of his own priestly role before God was based on the great Reformation text, "The just shall live by faith" (Romans 1:17). That awakening recovered the truth of "the priesthood of the believer." The privilege of access to God at a personal level was affirmed in Christ as people rediscovered their right to come to God with no need for a human mediator of divine blessing (1 Timothy 2:5). The bridge building idea in "priest" was revived. Priesthood was seen as a personal, practical privilege.

With praise to God for what that era recovered, I believe we're ripe for a new reformation concerning the believer's priestly ministry. I see an awakening about to extend the practical potential of our priestly function as believers. Five hundred years ago, the issue was *relationship*—restoring personal access *to* God. Today it is *worship*—revealing the potential in our praises *before* God.

Priests Who Reign

The Word of God directly links the two offices of king and priest, merging them into one and calling every believer to function in that joint role: "To Him who loved us and washed us from our sins in His own blood, and has made us kings and priests to His God and Father, to Him *be* glory and dominion forever and ever. Amen" (Revelation 1:5–6).

The importance of our being awakened to this dual calling—priestly kings/kingly priests—is that it places *worship* at the heart of God's program for restoring man's dominion. Our role as worshipping priests is the means to our role as reigning kings: "But you *are* a chosen generation, a royal priesthood, a holy nation, His own special people, that you may proclaim the praises of Him who called you out of darkness into His marvelous light (1 Peter 2:9).

The words "kingdom" and "royal" in this text clearly indicate a *regal* aspect to the priestly ministry of worship. Thus, at the core of our life in Christ is a summons to recognize that our dominion *in* Him correlates directly to our worship *of* Him. God's original plan that Israel become "a kingdom of priests" (Exodus 19:6)—a plan that was short-circuited when His people rejected it at Sinai—is now fulfilled in the Church. The priestly mission to lead the nations of the world to God by *becoming a people of worship* has been reissued.

We are only just beginning to again understand the *power of worship* to accomplish God's will. Today's *new reformation* is comprised of people just beginning to learn that Kingdom dominion—the rule of God's almighty power—comes as God responds to the worship of His people: "For the eyes of the Lord run to and fro throughout the whole earth, to show

Himself strong on behalf of *those* whose heart *is* loyal to Him" (2 Chronicles 16:9).

God's response to our worship is not a case of His demonstrating His power just because we make Him "feel good." Worship is not the stroking of a juvenile divine ego, nor is it the practice of a priestly magic, eliciting marvelous, cosmic powers. What the priest-king role of worship does is build a bridge between heaven's throne and earth's need. Worship welcomes God's rule into man's circumstances. Because we, the redeemed, are privileged to be the ones exercising the action that issues that welcome, God Himself ascribes to us a regal role. It is again as it was in the beginning—man may regain his assignment to rule because he has reclaimed his responsibility to worship.

The early believers were first to discover the priority of worship as the key to recovering world dominion under God's will. They were at worship when the first great breakthrough in global evangelism took place. "Now in the church that was at Antioch there were certain prophets and teachers. ... As they ministered to the Lord and fasted, the Holy Spirit said, 'Now separate to Me Barnabas and Saul for the work to which I have called them.' Then, having fasted and prayed, and laid hands on them, they sent *them* away" (Acts 13:1–3).

This thrusting forth of those two men from Antioch is as striking an event as any in the Scriptures. It shaped the world forever and set the direction of history's flow. It occasioned the turning of a corner into an era of Kingdom expansion that continues to this day. However, what we often fail to notice is that this small group's strategy for global missionary enterprise was not the product of human ingenuity. It was born simply as humble believers sought God in worship, fulfilling a priest's ministry described since Aaron's time as "ministering to the Lord."[1]

This may be the hour the Church most needs this reforming truth.

With the technological, media, and mechanical resources available, there is a greater temptation than ever for spiritual leaders and congregations to attempt to accomplish the work of God by the resources of man. There has always been a frightening tendency to mechanize spiritual enterprise in our zeal to achieve more for God's Kingdom. However, the Holy Spirit is emphasizing something else today. He is directing our appointment to priestly worship for the release of Kingdom advancement. He is enlisting a new contingent of priests; calling *every* believer anew to dynamic worship.

We should not fear answering that call, nor think it means to no longer act practically or sensibly. The priestly mission to worship is not to resign responsible duty, but to acknowledge that whatever we seek to *do* for God cannot exceed what we are to *be* before Him.

What He's called us to *first* is priests—"praisers!"

> In Him also we have obtained an inheritance, being predestined according to the purpose of Him who works all things according to the counsel of His will, that we who first trusted in Christ should be to the praise of His glory (Ephesians 1:11–12).

> You also, as living stones, are being built up a spiritual house, a holy priesthood, to offer up spiritual sacrifices acceptable to God through Jesus Christ (1 Peter 2:5).

It is difficult, without seeming rather mystical, to elaborate on how the "bridge building" ministry of priestly worship and praise is the most practical thing today's Church can learn. Someone is sure to think misty-eyed worshipping will replace clear-headed thinking. That can happen, of course, but it isn't God's way and it certainly isn't my point.

Through worship we can access the finest of everything, for there is now a route between the invisible and the visible. When God invades the scene of our praise and visits us with His grace and power, He will not overlook obvious basics:

1. Such worship is not a substitute for the teaching and preaching of the Word. It does precede it, however, and sometimes is entwined with it. In that way worship expands the possibilities of preaching, because it establishes an atmosphere of responding to God's will. Worship ignites, illuminates and unveils the revelation of Scripture. The truth *lives* among us!
2. Such worship is not an attempt to escape attention to administrative practicality or mundane responsibility. Still, when we learn to frame our business day in worship, discovering the importance of preceding all with praise (as opposed to a quick "bless us" prayer), we find that we can be remarkably more efficient.

I think a broader awareness of the believer's priesthood *in worship* is a fulfillment of certain Old Testament prophecies given by Ezekiel and Jeremiah.

Don't Sweat It

"Thou shalt not sweat it!"

I chuckled at the punchline given by the voice on the phone. A fellow pastor had posed the setup question, "Have you heard the Eleventh Commandment?"

Roy Hicks and I had been talking about our joyous experiences since both our congregations were growing so miraculously—his in Eugene, Oregon, and mine in Southern California. What humbled us both was how it had all occurred so rapidly and so easily, without promotion or fanfare on our part. We were very conscious of the fact a renewal in worship was at the heart of it. That was the context of his "Eleventh Commandment" crack.

It was a direct reference to our mutual concern that we not get in God's way. Our mutual background and experience inclined us both toward energetic promotionalism. But having begun to find a better way—God's way—we felt cautious that neither of us become even inadvertently guilty of substituting "sweat" for the priestly service of praise to God.

Roy's remark came from an explicit directive that God gave Ezekiel. It concerned the clothing to be worn by those priests who would serve God's Temple at a future day: "they shall not clothe themselves with *anything that* causes sweat" (Ezekiel 44:18).

Commentators differ widely on the meaning and timing of Ezekiel's predictions of a final Temple to be built unto God in the last times.[2] However, none preempt a present fulfillment of the prophet's vision in its immediate, spiritual sense. The stream of blessing that Ezekiel saw bursting from under the Temple threshold is clearly a forecast of a great river of refreshing at the last times. Some students believe it is one of the texts Jesus was alluding to as He spoke of the breaking forth in "rivers of living water" (John 7:38), when He would come and fill every believer with the Holy Spirit.

Jeremiah elaborates the same concept of a worldwide dimension of blessing—a "flowing together" of people in praise at a great future time of visitation: "Therefore they shall come and sing in the height of Zion, Streaming to the goodness of the Lord … Their souls shall be like a well-watered garden, and they shall sorrow no more at all" (Jeremiah 31:12).

In New Testament terms, the reference to Zion does not require a pilgrimage to Jerusalem. The words of Ezekiel and Jeremiah clearly relate to today. The writer of Hebrews places *every* believer in "Zion," *every time* we worship: "For you have not come to [Sinai] … But you have come to Mount Zion and to the city of the living God, the heavenly Jerusalem … to Jesus the Mediator of the new covenant" (Hebrews 12:18–24).

This prophesied priestly awakening, which is a very real formation, is occasioning a breakthrough in ministry and spiritual results. The Holy Spirit of God is teaching us the way to move all ministry beyond mere activities—those sweat-generating pursuits of fruitless tradition and soul-wearying churchmanship.

Much Work—Much Worship

I was so stirred on this theme, and the Holy Spirit gave me a powerful analogy with which to exhort our congregation:

"God has given us *much work* to do as a people. Therefore, our foremost task is to become a people of *much worship*. We must precede all and all must proceed with *worship*. Biblical terminology calls a congregation a 'body,' and, as a 'body,' we would be wise to pursue our mission in the light of a practical point related to 'bodies.' Bodies perspire. It has nothing to do with sin; it's just our physical nature. Nevertheless, I think that suggests a lesson about worship.

"Church 'bodies' tend to labor with perspiration-producing earnestness. That's no sin either. However, before *all* our bodies, worship is the fragrance with which we must cover ourselves. Just as a human body appropriately prepares itself with colognes, deodorants, and perfumes—lest the unpleasantness of the natural odor produced by working cause the body to become objectionable—so the Body of the Church must precede its God-appointed tasks with the sweet, supernatural savor and incense of worship. It's our only security against the 'smell of the flesh' tainting the atmosphere wherein God seeks to display His glory."

Worship is basic to the most rapid advancement of the Kingdom of God. It is central because *Kingdom* power is never generated by the energy of the flesh but is released by the power of the Holy Spirit. The priestly ministry of the believer is crucially necessary because our dominion as *kings* rises from our worship as *priests* and because it makes room for God's miracle power without leaving a place for "flesh" to rush to seek the glory. It welcomes the Holy Spirit's distributing of gifts while avoiding Corinthian carnality or confusion.

Such statements reflect a growing grasp of God's Word, and this is fueling the fires of a reformation in worship—a recognition that what began over five centuries ago has not exhausted the richness of the meaning inherent in the words, "the priesthood of the believer." With the new awakening to priestly ministry, Christians everywhere are opening up to allow for a biblical release in worship. As they do, it seems a new era of evangelism is beginning to take place. Worship is garnering a harvest!

Leighton Ford described his amazement at a discovery he made in India, where unbelievers were opening their homes at the request of Christians, "That we might use your house for a worship service." With that request, homes opened out of interest and curiosity, with the results that many have received the gospel. The amazing thing was that their readiness to do so was based on their merely seeing Christians worshipping the Lord.

Mrs. David Watson, wife of the late beloved rector in York, England, has employed an unusual worship tactic. She trained and led groups of the congregation's children, who often made their way through the park near their church *dancing* their praise to God! As a result, many outsiders' have been immediately attracted to the church service—even as the children danced in childlike abandon. Once there, the visitors experienced the congregation at worship and were led to salvation.

Youth With A Mission has taken worship teams into the streets of Amsterdam, where the jaded tastes of the worldly wise, carnally sated, and intellectually defiant have proven resistant to the claims of the gospel. Yet, as worshippers have simply lifted their voices in song, hearts have often melted before God as the Holy Spirit invaded the marketplace where worship had prepared a place for His workings.

In our own congregation, there are frequent occasions when I have followed an extended period of worship and praise with a simple invitation to receive Christ. It is not uncommon to experience a dozen or more people at a time opening up to the love of God and growing in Christ—drawn by the Holy Spirit working through the spirit of worship.

The remarkable thing about these examples is that they do not involve especially skilled performances. Of course, the musicians practiced and the dancing children rehearsed, but these occasions did not feature the unusually gifted as, for example, at a gospel music concert. As valid as the latter may be in evangelism, that is not what I am describing. I'm talking about the sheer power of praise and worship to introduce the rule of God's Kingdom power, which deeply touches hearts, and manifests delivery and salvation.

Priests and Kings—At Home

Believers are beginning to learn the power of worship in the everyday routine of their personal lives. It's not only contributing to the rise of homes filled with a holy happiness, but homes where the presence of God's Kingdom crowds out the efforts of hell to erode peace and unity of families.

Chuck was attending one of the Men's Growth Seminars we conduct each month. I had taught on the power of praise as a man's means for exercising his priestly role as spiritual leader of his home. I based my talks on God's word to Abraham—to walk through the length and breadth of the land promised him (Genesis 13:17). I proposed that as Abraham's spiritual sons (Galatians 3:29; Romans 4:12-18), we should do the same thing.

"How about walking the boundaries of your property, however large or small it may be? As the priest-leader of your family, sing the praise of the Lord as you do it. Welcome the rule of His Kingdom to reign over all and throughout all your household."

Chuck went home and shared the teaching with Judy and decided to take this simple truth in the literal way I had proposed—to apply it with worshipping faith to their situation. They had been having a real problem with one of their teenage daughters and had come to the end of their own ability to deal with the situation. The next day Chuck rose before daylight—not wanting their neighbors to see what he was doing and think him foolish or superstitious. With songful praise and worship, he circled the perimeter of his lot, believing that God's timeless ways apply today.

"Later that day," Judy said, "while I was working in the kitchen, I felt the strongest prompting to go to Katy's room. As I walked down the hall, praying for her, I felt directed to open the top right-hand drawer of her dresser and reach to the back, beneath the things in the drawer. I did so, and without probing at all—simply doing as I felt directed—my hand came upon a cellophane bag. When I removed it, I was shocked. It contained marijuana."

Without detailing the story further, the thrilling outcome centered in Katy's response that evening after school when Chuck and Judy confronted her—she began weeping and expressing her gratitude to God for leading her mom to the package.

"Mom. Dad. You can't know how happy I am this happened! You know I've never done anything like this and I didn't want to now. I know I've been giving you trouble, but not this bad.

"One of the kids at school gave me that bag to get me to consider trying it. Even though I didn't, I did keep it. I knew it was all wrong, but in my rebellion I thought that if I kept it available I might decide later to risk it."

Between sobs she went on to welcome her parents' prayers with her as she confessed this and other sins. On the spot, she returned to an obedient walk with Christ. For Chuck and Judy's part, it's all simply a case of the power of worship and praise when introduced into the home.

Is this kind of thing superstition? Coincidence? Fanaticism?

Not at all! Not when the spiritual intent of the old covenant's priestly ministry has been transferred to New Testament believers as we've studied.

If Aaron's bearing the family names of the tribes upon his shoulders before the Lord every day held intercessory significance with God then, the glory of the New Covenant holds at least as much for those who come with worship and name their family daily before the heavenly throne (Exodus 28:12).

If Aaron's rushing with incense into the midst of the plague of judgment actually stopped its spread (Numbers 16:46–50), it's not unlikely or presumptuous to expect today that the incense of God's people at prayer and worship could effect a reversal of the destruction ripping cities and nations apart (Revelation 5:8; James 5:16–18).

Today, the reformation truth of "the priesthood of the believer" is growing and reaching higher. It is expanding worship as the concept is understood—built on the solid ground of God's Word. More believers are coming to relish and respond to the wealth of meaning in their priestly function, as they see praise and worship being applied with priestly effectiveness.

Worship has the power to penetrate hearts, for its childlike beauty and authenticity bypass resistant minds and touch souls with the tender reality of God's presence.

Worship has the power to neutralize the power of demonic attack upon the people of God, for, wherever the spirit of praise resides, God is exalted and neither flesh nor devil can successfully perpetuate their designs.

The New Reformation in worship is advancing. The royal priesthood of the believer in Christ is beginning to accomplish what it was ordained to do—extend God's rule through worship.

This is bridge building—spanning the limits of man's circumstance and, with worship, welcoming the entry of God's unlimited rulership. It's a new government bringing the Spirit of life into a decaying world. This reformation is causing a revolution that, similar to another one before it, is seeking "to secure the blessings of liberty to ourselves and our posterity." Those words were written by men willing to experience a revolution in order to extend that blessing.

The new reformation in worship invites us to one also.

8

Sam's Song
of Renewal's Ways

"Let all the past be but a holy prelude, Lord,
To the mighty fire and power You now outpour on me.
All consuming flame come and overflow me,
And let Thy Kingdom come unto me this hour."
J.W.H.

THE MOST UNSUNG hero of the Old Testament is Samuel.

He bridged two eras—from the judges to the kings.

He lived in purity while a declining priest bred a decadent household.

He immortalized obedience in the midst of a relativistic society, and …

He ordained the king destined to sire the Messiah and foreshadow His rule.

Samuel is a study in simple obedience without fanfare, of commitment without apparent reward, and of faithfulness to duty when no one else much understood or cared.

Samuel is a study in the ways of transition—of renewal. Hannah was tortured by barrenness—the affliction of childlessness that caused any ancient Hebrew woman to doubt her worth and wonder about her favor with God. Though well-loved by her husband Elkanah, she longed for a child.

This brought her near despair, and as so often is the case when human beings turn to God in their plight, that despair begat a song of hope. It began with prayer and became music.

God answered her prayer for a child, and upon Hannah's next visit to the Tabernacle—now situated in Shiloh since Israel had entered the land nearly three hundred years before—she worshipped the Lord and said:

> My heart rejoices in the Lord;
> My horn is exalted in the Lord.
> I smile at my enemies,
> Because I rejoice in Your salvation.
> No one is holy like the Lord,
> For *there is* none besides You,
> Nor *is there* any rock like our God (1 Samuel 2:1–2)

Her song wings on for a full ten verses in the second chapter of 1 Samuel, preserved there by her son's pen as a commemoration of his own birth. One might call it *Sam's Song*, the melody of a woman whose God reversed her situation.

Revolution.

Samuel is an example of God at work doing that. Just as surely as Samuel was an instrument of Israel's turning from an era of political and moral lawlessness during the time of the Judges, and returning from the spiritual emptiness during Eli's high priestly rule, *Sam's Song* connotes God's ways to cause a revolution.

Renewal. Resurrection. Restoration.

These are key words in God's methods of reordering things. Human revolutions may change an existing order, but they usually carry the excess baggage of bitterness, resentment, retaliation, and bloodletting. Instead, when we tune in to Hannah's song, as she revels in her restoration from barrenness, God reminds us that "by strength no man shall prevail," and that the Lord is the One who "lifts the beggar from the ash heap to set him among princes and make him inherit the throne of glory" (1 Samuel 2:8).

The components of Hannah's situation—Samuel's birth and Israel's movement toward the king that God had in mind—may be quite similar to ours. Just as Hannah longed for a birth, I've met so many who truly long for spiritual renewal. Similarly, as her child led the way in the anointing of God's chosen King, David, so those seeking renewal are on track to realize a new entrance into God's Kingdom with love and power. Our examining of this parallel holds worthwhile lessons.

Samuel's life and leadership style reveal at least three points to teach any of us God's ways into renewal.

The Difficulty in Renewal

A person's *passion* for renewal and its practical *possibility* are often far apart and radically different. It's one thing to hunger for a reformation and another to have one. Not everyone enjoys the possibilities that I did when I came to an almost nonexistent congregation of eighteen members whose average age was over sixty years.

Although I was a young pastor, I enjoyed a good reputation in my denomination, and this disposed the handful of members I inherited in my favor. Because of this I experienced virtual hands-off freedom in leading them forward. No substantial built-in structures obstructed the path. I was hopeful of discovering the possibilities in the ministry of worship. They were so few in number that they were glad to have a pastor at all.

Moreover, they were not a resistant people anyway, so resistance was out of the question.

That is rarely the case.

I constantly meet pastors and laymen who recognize that a worship reformation is in progress and want to be a part of it. They are motivated by more than novelty or a quest for success. They genuinely want to be center-stream to the flow of the Holy Spirit in today's Church. However …

They face resistance.

Sometimes it's only in pockets of the congregation they love. At other times, it comes from the grass roots throughout every level of leadership in the church. Sometimes it's possible to discuss the subject of the congregation's need for renewal. Other times such discussion is deemed the equivalent of challenging the truth of the Virgin Birth. What can you do when you're in such a dilemma? First, we can always find support in the Lord, just as Hannah did.

God has a heart for people who hunger for renewal.

His faithfulness will always pour forth the fulfilling answer to those who "hunger and thirst after righteousness." Still, it is important to remember that whenever others' readiness does not match ours, He is their God also. His patience with those who fear renewal—even those who resist it—will often require His waiting longer than you or I want to wait. So many of us want to "get on with it" *right now!* However, we should consider the difference in God's *renewing* ways and man's *revolutionary* ones. Samuel's life is a good study in the spirit of faithfulness exhibited by someone who longed to see God's rule instituted, but who had to wait to see it accomplished in God's way.

Be Childlike, Not Chiding

The story of Samuel's boyhood breathes a quality of childlikeness worthy of our emulation. At a very early age, Hannah and Elkanah brought Samuel and dedicated him to the service of the Tabernacle. Under Eli's training and care, Samuel was subject to the high priest for several years of his early life—years marked by little other than his mother's annual gift to him of a new robe. It was a miniature ephod—a priestly order of garb designed for his ministry before the Lord.

During this same season of years, Eli's sons were living corruptly; despoiling pure worship at the Tabernacle, seducing women who came there, and stealing to serve their own greed and gluttony by taking from the sacrifices people brought. Worst of all, they disrespectfully rejected their aged father's repeated efforts at correcting them.

Eli, weakened from severe obesity, weariness of years, and despair over his rebellious sons, seems to epitomize any situation needing renewal. At the same time, Samuel is a clear picture of the new—the freshly available, God-ordained rule of the Holy Spirit that makes any renewal possible.

If ever a situation needed a head-on collision with revolution, this was one. However, God's wisdom and patience, modeled in Samuel, may teach us if we'll listen—the way to renewal is to be childlike, not chiding. He points our way to influencing a reformation without grumping about its need or thumping our discerning perspective on it.

There is a distinct grace in being able to continue in the middle of a situation that needs revival, deliverance, or salvation, while remaining both tender in heart and constant in growth. Something about Hannah's year-to-year gift of a new robe for

Samuel, joined to the phrase "but Samuel ministered before the Lord, even as a child," presents us with a lesson in patience. God does not require our assistance to force Him into situations that seem to have crowded Him out. He only needs someone who will continue to keep freshly robed for worship—those who, with simplicity of heart, remain constant in worship before God, regardless of what around them is polluted or dying.

I have often had dear people come to me who are troubled at the absence of spiritual vitality in the congregation they attend, indicating how deeply they desire revival. I understand their heart and their plight, and my counsel is that they learn from Samuel.

Brokenhearted husbands or wives describe to me the very real pain and agony of their discouraging marital situations, hoping against hope for a change and wondering if some gracious exit is allowable. I care about their pain and understand their concern. Nevertheless, I always encourage them to try Samuel's style of waiting and growing individually, before they surrender to discouragement or hasten out the doorway of divorce.

Renewal is not something solely needed by churches.

People need renewal.

Marriages need renewal.

Job situations need renewal.

Dozens of other human circumstances need revival.

The flesh is impatient. Revolution, not renewal, is too often its choice. Our flesh wants action, even if it's at the expense of pain. We're inclined to consider it an acceptable trade-off—simply exchanging one kind of pain for another. We are willing to take our lumps in hope that our revolution will secure a new day of God's way, but too easily we get our way instead, and apparent victory becomes only another kind of defeat. What renewal might have brought with time, revolution demolished in its carnal zeal for speedy results.

The way to avoid this delusion is to wait in worship.

One of the great principles of worship is that it gains dominion not by the force of self-assertion but by the power of praise. Worship wins because it is willing to sacrifice its comfort and its convenience and to make room for God to work by His might and in His time.

Samuel's first lesson in renewal is that the childlike, worshipping believer—who keeps renewed from season to season through a fresh robing of his own soul in the spirit of faith, hope, and love—*will eventually see renewal.* As Hannah did for Samuel, the Holy Spirit will provide ongoing newness if we'll allow Him. In the meantime, as Samuel with Eli, we might be disappointed over things that continue without change and we may weary over those in authority, who seem without the boldness to change what needs to be changed. Still, the soul who waits in worship before the throne of God will remain at peace and be fulfilled in the meantime. He will never be without the confidence that the Lord ultimately is in full control. The old hymn puts it:

> God is still on the throne,
> and He will remember His own.
> Though trials may press us
> and burdens distress us,
> He never will leave us alone.
> God is still on the throne,
> He never forsaketh His own.
> His promise is true,
> He will not forget you;
> God is still on the throne.[1]

Chiding may provoke action and force something that looks like victory. Childlikeness is the only way to insure that we actually will win.

Ichabod Is Only a Name

Church traditions might be termed "indeterminately spiritual." That is, a given tradition might be dynamically valid in one setting and not in another. It is not a case of validity—like beauty being in the eye of the beholder—but of true power issuing solely from the hand of God. Thus, if church tradition has lost its contact with God, it becomes a mere formality, for God's touch is no longer on it.

However, it is a mistake to assume that any tradition is devoid of dynamic power just because we don't see any power there now. Almost any practice that had once been an avenue of God's dynamic power is always a potential scene of holy lightning striking again. It's wise never to mock traditions, because you never know when you may need to see tradition activated for real and holy purposes!

This brings us to the Ark of the Covenant.

During Samuel's time, the Ark was the central feature of Israel's worship. It was placed in the Holy of Holies, the inner sanctum of the Tabernacle, and it contained the Ten Commandments, a commemorative portion of the manna, and Aaron's rod that had budded. The whole of it was covered with a small, solid gold platform called The Mercy Seat, upon which the blood of atonement was presented each year. If there were any question as to whether this "traditional" box had any power connected to it, those in Samuel's time remembered that where the Ark was, the presence and power of God had been manifest in the past.

However, something had happened—something bad.

As we have already noted, a high priest—whose physical condition seemed to bespeak his spiritual neglect—had proven ineffective at maintaining God's order in his own home. His sons, to whom his priesthood was bequeathed, had sorely corrupted their ways and totally ignored the holy standards of the Lord. Although worship *forms* were still the same, there was *no power* present. Israel had again become defenseless before her enemies—since God is the only real defense any of His people have. If they lose their vital touch with Him, they lose touch with the source of all their hope, purpose, and power.

The events that followed were a further commentary on the barrenness of spiritual leadership at that time. Eli's sons bear the Ark into battle. The Israelite troops are defeated again. The Philistines capture the Ark. They slay Eli's sons and Eli dies from a fall brought on by the shock of hearing the report of such a humiliating defeat and horrible disaster—The Ark … lost!

The whole scenario occasioned the naming of a baby—one of the best-known names in the Bible: Ichabod.

He was Eli's grandson, born prematurely on the day the Ark of the Covenant was captured. His mother went into early labor upon hearing of the death of her husband and died in delivery, but not without naming the newborn boy, "Call him Ichabod— the glory has departed from Israel!"

Chabod is the Hebrew word for "glory." It refers to the idea of *weight* more than to the "something shiny" that we connect with the meaning of "glory." In essence, the idea of glory relates to the *substance*, the *reality* of a person, practice or institution. The "glory" has to do with what it is that causes a thing to excel beyond its counterparts. For Israel, the "glory" was the presence of the Lord. He was the One who offered them qualities of excellence as a people and powers of excellence in battle. However, a battle had been lost, and the dying woman's cry, which labeled her son with a less-than-desired name—Ichabod, or "no glory"—was half-right. The glory had departed, but not simply because of the capturing of the Ark. God's real power in Israel's midst had departed well before that, but Samuel's rising ministry held promise of a recovery.

There are several lessons to learn in this part of Samuel's life story.

1. We never need fear that the disappearance of God's power and presence from among a people necessarily will dilute His purpose or destiny for us. Samuel's life and destiny were not hindered by the sagging spiritual conditions or the disastrous events of that day. He walked with and worshipped God, and God's purpose for him was fulfilled. When we do the same, we will experience the same.

2. Merely sustaining religious forms and formulas argues neither for the presence nor for the absence of God's blessing and power. However, it is certain that into every situation of spiritual accountability a day of crisis will come. When it does, truth will be known and sham will be exposed. Neither you nor I need to force the showdown. God will take care of it in His time and by His means.

3. When "Ichabod" is pronounced over a situation, it is important to know that the absent glory does not reveal an absent God. God is never absent, even when the spiritual emptiness of those still exercising once-mighty forms of worship prevent His display of power now.

It is this last point I am most interested in making, for there is an unfortunate habit of spiritually inclined people either to demean traditions or demand too much of them. On the one hand, some are quick to deny the worth of *any* form. On the other, some expect the exercise of religious forms to mandate God's response. The "Ichabod" of God may appear to apply to a practice, a place, or a people, but it is unwise for you or me to say as much. God is often much more present and ready to work than people realize. Don't embarrass yourself by pronouncing the demise of His operations at a place or in a situation where you have given up. Remember this, especially when tempted to criticize those who maintain a firm liturgy in their worship.

It's also a mistake to think that only high church or Catholic celebrants conduct a liturgy. A liturgy is any order of service, and even the absence of one, or a flexibility in order, as practiced in the worship of more casual or spontaneous groups. All this is an order in its own right. Every liturgy is the fruit of a history lived out by a people who sought God and found Him. They used those methods of worship at the beginning because they had found something in His Word that sparked their response, and thereby shaped their practice. However, as is so often the case, given time, forms prevail and purposes become forgotten. The "weight of glory" may thereby be drained from the practice, not because the liturgical practice was useless, but simply because the perfunctory exercise of meaningless motions provides no resting place for the weight of God's glory.

Be assured of this, however: if hungry and thirsty hearts will again search the Word and seek the Lord, an "Ichabod" spirit cannot prevail. In ancient Israel, God may have refused to bless a sinning people with victory over the Philistines. However, when those same Philistines foolishly believe they have added the Lord to their pantheon of deities in Dagon's temple, they find out differently. When Samuel rises to worship, God speaks again.

No, the "glory" of Israel *had not* departed. God was and is still alive and ready to display His power. He's simply searching for those who will meet the conditions.

Enter David.

The Promise of "Kingdom"

Samuel is called the kingmaker, because he anointed the first two kings of Israel. He anointed both at God's command—the first, because God permitted the will of the people, and the second, because God's will was being done.

Saul is the greatest tragedy of Old Testament history.

He's the country boy who had his chance at greatness, started well, became puffed with pride, and turned into a malicious, demon-guided demagogue who, shamed by his enemies, died in battle. David started the same way Saul did: a strapping shepherd boy also from the hill country. There is little difference in David's story in its details. Both he and Saul won early victories. Both were heralded first by part of the people and later by all the people. However, there is a radical and central difference in their personalities: David had a *heart* for God.

In learning lessons from Samuel about renewal, perhaps distinguishing between Saul and David is our most important assignment. You and I may apply the first two lessons drawn from Sam's Song:

1. We should wait with patience and walk in worship as God grows His purpose in us, refusing to force the issue of "change" and wait for God's time.

2. We should remember that the secret of renewal lies not in a particular form, or absence of one, but that God's glory waits to visit and fill those who hunger and thirst for Him.

However, if we learn these points well and miss the third, we are in danger of finding the *beginning* of God's "kingdom power" and still miss its continuing. We must be wise at this point, for *continuous* promise and blessing is the objective of God's rule. Historic incidents or sporadic occurrences are no substitute for an "increase of His government and peace which knows no end" (Isaiah 9:7 author's paraphrase). It is a hard fact that the *appearance* of renewal is far easier to produce than the solid *actuality*. A more demanding truth is this: the *actuality* of renewal does not guarantee its *continuity*. Consequently, the seeker after renewal must learn these two disciplines:

1. *Let the Lord give rise to* His *kingdom demonstration.* Israel's pursuit of a king on their terms brought Saul into the picture. We are no less capable of conjuring up a renewal that looks like God's will and isn't.
2. *Prioritize the "heart" rather than outward appearances.* We see this in God's Word, as Samuel speaks at the anointing of David: "Man looks at the outward appearance, but the Lord looks at the heart" (1 Samuel 16:7).

The maintenance of a right heart only requires that our quest be solely for God and unto His glory. The Lord promised David that the Messiah would issue from his line and that God would ensure that there would always be a king on David's throne. This promise was based on David's *heart* relationship with God— sustained blessing always is.

True renewal *comes* where hearts wait for God.

True renewal *manifests* where hearts thirst for God.

True renewal *stays* where hearts walk with God.

Hannah's song set the theme for her son's life: "He lifts up ... He gives strength ... He exalts." Samuel learned that song and lived out its wisdom. Another man learned it from him, and made Sam's Song the theme of a hundred more. He led Israel to a place where her worship brought her to victories unsurpassed in all her history. He learned to link the worship of God with the expansion of His rule through His people. He did both wholeheartedly and victoriously.

His name was David.

9

Boards and Big Wheels Won't Make It

And to the angel of the church in Philadelphia write,
"These things says He who is holy, He who is true,
'He who has the key of David.'"
Revelation 3:7

IT IS NOT by coincidence that Israel's highest development in worship and her broadest boundaries of government came at the same time.

David was the leader during both.

The shepherd boy, who strummed and sang to his sheep, rose to rule a nation and taught God's flock to sing God's praise. The youthful slayer of Goliath, whose heroism stirred an army to boldness, came to the throne, and led Israel's warriors in vanquishing their enemies. There is no more insightful study of worship than the life and music of David.

In worship he soars, and with worship he wars.

The union of the two seems paradoxical, but this king seemed to have discerned God's heart. David knew that God wanted to dwell among His people to bless, to give victory, and to shower His mercy and lovingkindness upon them all. David represents the very practical potential in broadening horizons of worship. He forges a bold union between worship and warfare, between loving God and wanting His blessing, between exalting the Lord and asking for His help. He bypasses the traditional theological inclinations so prevalent today against such raw requests as bless me, help me, heal me, prosper me. For many of us, such direct petitions aren't quite spiritual enough. Today's ecclesiastical convictions tend to render any hint at "seeking to be blessed" as being suspect of carnal motivation. Furthermore, the watching, listening, ever-critical worldly person scoffs, "If God *does* exist He's above hearing such mundane appeals from mere mankind."

David would please neither group. Nevertheless, in spite of that, God's Word has another assessment of him: "And when He [God] had removed him [Saul], He raised up for them David as king, to whom also He gave testimony and said, 'I have found David the son of Jesse, a man after My own heart, who will do all My will.'" (Acts 13:22).

When God Himself confers such a conclusive commendation on David, we can hardly challenge his approach to worship or fail to recognize its nobility. Whatever cheap or shallow misinterpretations of Scripture may today invite believers to charisma without character or to prosperity without propriety, David represented neither imbalance. Yet, David did experience abundance, success, and victory upon victory—and worship was at the heart of his movement into such bountiful living and leadership.

However, how did it start?

The Shaping of a Worship Leader

It would be impossible simply from his psalm references to gain a full understanding of David's discovery of an intimate relationship with God. However, he *does* model that.

He does it with intimacy, along with emotion.

David exhibits qualities of heart and practices in praise that make us accountable to the truth they reveal. A high view of the Scriptures requires a dual acknowledgment that today's "reformed" worship must face. Two facts—God's testimony to David's understanding of His own heart, and the Holy Spirit's will to include so many of David's worship psalms in the Eternal Word—join to force us to deal with these conclusions:

1. God not only is unopposed to emotional worship; He welcomes it.
2. God not only allows the worshipper's plea for success; He rewards it.

There is no evidence that David had a structured agenda for applying these facts, as though he "knew all along that God is like this" or that he thought he could manipulate the Almighty to serve his own private interests. None at all. However, there is a clear report in the revelation of God's Word, and there are net results to total. Between these two facts there unfolds the shaping of a man who led his people to worship God at even greater heights.

The public beginnings of that leadership in worship took place after David had conquered Jerusalem. Having established his capital city, David longed to bring back the Ark of the Covenant to a tabernacled center where Israel could again come and seek God. His approach to that mission is most instructive.

The Tabernacle of David

The Tabernacle raised in Moses' time seems to disappear sometime between Joshua and David. It's an interesting puzzle for

Bible students to attempt to solve. After its establishment in Shiloh, following Israel's entry into the land (ca. 1400 B.C.), the Tabernacle is mentioned only four times. After the loss of the Ark of the Covenant to the Philistines during Eli's high priesthood (ca. 1150 B.C.), it seems that the absence of the very object that made the Tabernacle necessary and gave reason for its existence, occasioned its virtual demise. During Samuel's ministry, he operates from more than one worship center, which apparently confirms that the Tabernacle was probably not in active use. [1]

In the meantime, the Philistines had returned the Ark of the Covenant. After having captured it, they discovered to their dismay that Yahweh was not a dime store deity to be toyed with or to be added to a pantheon of conquered tribal gods. He was the Lord Jehovah, God of all creation, and Israel's Savior. The story of the plague upon their cities and the embarrassment of their god, Dagon, simply because of the presence of the Ark of the Covenant, would be humorous if it weren't so disastrous for them and so laden with lessons for us. For over twenty years, the Ark had been in the village of Kirjath Jearim, where it rested at the household of a man named Abinadab.

It is at this point we hear with a story—a set of events that at once reveal David's humanness, anger, and capacity for misjudgment, as well as his heart for God, passion for His presence, and humility before the Lord (2 Samuel 6; 1 Chronicles 13–16).

David's Heart for God

There is a fundamental prerequisite for everyone who would worship God or lead others to do so. David abundantly manifests that quintessential trait of a heart filled with a passion for God: "My soul thirsts for You; my flesh longs for You In a dry and thirsty land Where there is no water. So I have looked for You in the sanctuary, to see Your power and Your glory" (Psalm 63:1–2).

David reveals a largeness of heart here, which not only desires God's working in his own life, but also longs for His manifest glory "in the sanctuary." The deep cry of such a leader's soul for *both* his own need *and* that of his people will never go unrewarded. In the text we're examining, David called the people to join him in that quest: "If *it seems* good to you and if it is of the Lord our God … let us bring the ark of our God back to us" (1 Chronicles 13:2–3).

His objective was to bring the Ark to Jerusalem, for David valued the worship of God. He knew the priceless worth of God's presence that always attends those who worship Him, and he prepared a new place for the Ark of God to dwell: "So they brought the ark of God, and set it in the midst of the tabernacle that David had erected for it" (1 Chronicles 16:1).

Upon the Ark's arrival, David conducted a great feast—a magnanimous event that beautifully illustrates that wherever worship is renewed, people will always be both filled with joy and fed. The celebration was also marked by David's introduction of several new songs for the occasion.

We don't know if David led the throng or if he sang the new songs himself. However, we do know that the music of praise and worship filled the feast-time. The Book of Chronicles gives us portions of at least three psalms that David had written to the Lord.[2] All this newness, feasting, and rejoicing with high praises to the Lord at the climax of the story, come only after experiencing considerable difficulty.

David's Humanness and Anger

Why in the world the idea was ever hatched is difficult to decide!

The only other time in history that the Ark of the Covenant had been carried on a cart was when the Philistines sent it back—fearful and unwilling even to be near it (1 Samuel 5:6). Obviously ignorant or forgetful of the fact that from the time of Moses the Lord had commanded that the Ark be carried on the shoulders of the priests, David built "a new cart, and brought it [the Ark] out of the house of Abinadab … and Uzzah and Ahio, the sons of Abinadab, drove the new cart" (2 Samuel 6:3). The fashioning of the cart is a classic example of man's sincerest efforts proving horribly out of synchronization with the divine order. David's capacity for human error glares forth—a rather comforting fact considering the eventual outcome, even though the immediate results were horribly tragic.

The great parade, planned to bring the Ark all the way to Jerusalem, hardly makes it out of town. When one of the oxen pulling the cart stumbles, the great gold-covered box starts to slide off the cart. Uzzah leaps forward to secure it from falling—and *is struck dead*! It's a sudden end to a great plan—a tragic conclusion to what had seemed the start of something big. It seems a bewildering judgment considering they were doing so much to attempt to honor God.

Moreover, David became angry.

He named the place "The breach of Uzzah!"[3], apparently feeling that a trust he felt he enjoyed with God had been breached. He became afraid, and his despair shouts forth in the cry, "How can I bring the Ark of God to me?" (1 Chronicles 13:12).

They parked the Ark on the nearest property. The parade ended. They buried Uzzah and David sulked back to Jerusalem, irritated and confused.

I have been so refreshed by the insights on this passage that two fellow pastors shared with me, I want to relay their observations. Their words taught me wisdom just at the time I was zealous of seeing a renewal in worship begun with my own people. Their insights into David's "worship leadership" might help you as much as they helped me.

Don Pickerill observed, "Look at David building the cart. Can we see ourselves in our dedicated diligence at church-work? How many times I've labored on the supposition that God's presence can be brought in on a 'new cart'—a new program of some kind. Do you know what carts are made of? *Boards and big wheels!*

"Have you ever tried it like I have? If we can just get enough 'boards'—teams of people working on the project, and big wheels—a celebrity or successful person here or there, then we can really get things going for God! Oh, how pitiful, Church. Boards and big wheels won't make it. God's presence travels on the shoulders of His priests—that is, on the praises of *all* His people, for *we* are the contemporary 'priests of God.' He doesn't need our new carts. He simply wants our priestly praise."

Jerry Cook was sharing from this passage: "Will you look at the names of the two brothers 'helping' the Ark along—Ahio and Uzzah. I was interested about this, and looking up the meaning of their names I discovered that Ahio means *"friendly"* and Uzzah means *"strength."* I couldn't help but laugh, because it was so symbolic of my earliest conceptions of the way ministry is to succeed, to 'roll the old cart along.'

"First, get an 'Ahio' out in front. You know—somebody loaded with personality—Mr. Friendly. We seem to think that what we need to really succeed is to cultivate a top quality PR approach—Public Relations. The closer to Madison Avenue, the better, right?

"Then, with PR, we need a backup. We need strength—people with drive, dynamism, and determination. Thus, what we can't accomplish by skill or personality we'll compensate for with brute strength. And we try so sincerely—so *very* sincerely—to bring the presence of God into our churches—and sadly the conclusion is so often much the same as here. The end of it all is *death*."

The words of them both sting with the bite of arctic air after sitting in a stuffy room. It became clear exactly why some of my past zeal for God had been so unproductive.

We who would welcome the presence of God into our beloved churches should learn from David's human error. We may need to repent for the bitterness or angry bewilderment we feel because God hasn't blessed our "new cart" efforts of the past with a visitation of His glory.

He is waiting to bless, but humble acceptance of His terms is the only way we can realize it.

David's Humility before God

There are few things more difficult to do than to admit we are wrong. It isn't so much our unwillingness to acknowledge failures or mistakes, but our fear that if we do so, no one will remember that we *meant* well even though we didn't do well.

David was willing to be wrong, and to start over.

After three months, a report reached him: the farmland of Obed-Edom, where the Ark had remained when Uzzah died, was being blessed with great fruitfulness. The message was clear—the problem wasn't because God didn't want to bless, the problem was with man knowing how to receive His blessing. Because of this report, David consulted Zadok and Abiathar, the leading priests. They explained to him the proper order. The pattern had apparently been overlooked because the Tabernacle was in disuse, and it had been so long since the priestly ministry had moved it. They had searched the scrolls, and discovered the message—the *Ark must be borne on the shoulders of the priests* (1 Chronicles 15:3–15). The issue is painfully clear—painful to the point of Uzzah's death and David's frustration. God doesn't need pushing. He calls for praise. God doesn't use programs. He uses people—people who worship Him!

The ensuing scene described in the text is aglow with a combination of new wisdom in worship and new rejoicing through praise:

1. Instead of percussion and stringed instruments as at the first attempt, the silver breath of trumpet-sound fills the air. (Could this contain a message on the difference between the work of our flesh and the breath of the Spirit?)
2. Instead of carnal efforts at securing God's reputation (Uzzah's attempt to balance the Ark), sacrifices are offered at regular intervals all the way to Jerusalem, fulfilling God's Word.
3. Instead of a vocally silent entourage, praiseless except for the musicians' best efforts and the accompanying hoof beats of oxen, this time the instrumental music is joined by the throng's "raising the voice with resounding joy."

There is great praising. Human concern for retaining an air of sophistication has been cast aside. In addition, as though to verify conclusively the childlike passion and purity of motive compelling his whole pursuit of God's glory, and his delight over anticipating broader blessing, David suddenly breaks into a dance.

It was not a casual affair.

The king himself, usually garbed in regal clothing befitting his office, lays aside his outer garments and begins to dance. We do not know the duration of his dancing, its tempo or its style. However, we do know that David was specifically rejoicing in the dance as *an act of humility* before God. He was ecstatic, to be sure—but he hadn't lost his mind. He'd found the presence of God!

The Ark came to Jerusalem!

"Listen," the dancer seems to be singing as he leads the way to a new Tabernacle, which he has prepared to receive the heavenly Visitor:

> Praise is awaiting You, O God, in Zion;
> And to You the vow shall be performed.
> O You who hear prayer,
> To You all flesh will come (Psalm 65:1–2).

Feasting will follow. Israel's boundaries will continue to enlarge. Worship will grow to dimensions yet unknown among the people, for a leader of worship is the leader of the people.

His heart for God is single, his human misjudgments dealt with, his humility before God a model for his people.

However, he will face one problem before nightfall.

There are always people who resist worship, because its price involves new and renewing lessons in humility.

There is always Michal.

10

Dancing Kings and Barren Queens

Once told at Yale is the story of a Harvard cheerleader
who, impeccably dressed in tie and tans, arose
to lead a yell; saying in a beautifully modulated voice,
"Come, deah students, let us give three cheeahs foah
deah old Hahvad—not so loud as to be boisterous,
but sufficient to demonstrate ouah enthusiasm!"

MICHAL WAS INFURIATED.

Her husband's partial disrobing before all his subjects—as
he stripped his royal outer garment to allow freedom for
dancing his praise to the Lord God of Israel—was, in her
opinion, inexcusable. David had actually worn a light linen
ephod—only a humble priestly smock when compared to
the apparel befitting his high office. She complained, "How
glorious was the king of Israel today, uncovering himself
today in the eyes of the maids of his servants, as one of the
base fellows shamelessly uncovers himself!" (2 Samuel 6:20).
An uninformed listener would have thought David guilty of
exhibitionism—of stark nudity and an obscene display, but
he had only danced in joyous praise to God.

Michal had watched it from the window of their home
as the procession drew near Jerusalem and toward the

Tabernacle that her husband had erected to welcome the Ark of God's covenant. Look! With *all* the people *watching*, David was "leaping and whirling before the Lord." The biblical record says that as she watched, "she despised him in her heart" (2 Samuel 6:16), and upon his arrival home that evening she unloaded on him. Now she was facing another kind of music—*barrenness*.

This story spells out a tale that has been told repeatedly, and one that today's reformation in worship demands be told once more. It's a message full of wisdom and warning—not a warning of impending divine judgment but of wisdom as to the implications of pride. It's a warning of what can happen when human tastes reject the childlike simplicity and practical humility at worship that please the Divine.

Barren. Childless. Unfruitful. Unproductive.

Those words all describe Michal from that encounter forward. Though she was married to the king, from the day she so scathingly assaulted her husband's worship, she "had no children to the day of her death" (2 Samuel 6:23). Scripture doesn't say if David rejected any conjugal relationship or if it was a curse that somehow came upon her. However, David had responded to her charges, "*It was* before the Lord, who chose me instead of your father and all his house, to appoint me ruler over the people of the Lord, over Israel. Therefore, I will play *music* before the Lord. And I will be even more undignified than this, and will be humble in my own sight" (2 Samuel 6:21–22).

One would have thought her heritage would have recommended more wisdom than Michal showed. She was daughter to the deposed King Saul. Her father had not only lost his throne, but before his death had shown hideous and unjustified jealousy and hatred toward David, who was guilty only of being a faithful warrior. Now with Saul's entire house overthrown by his own folly and defeat, his daughter Michal might well have suffered capital punishment as the remnant of a family known to be hostile to David. Yet David continues to show mercy by sparing her life. Michal will live, but she will live a cardboard existence, bereft of all the joys that might have been.

My Majesty in the Mirror

I have grown unable to read that story without thinking about our human preoccupation with dignity, and remembering a brutal confrontation God brought me to with this problem in my own heart. Allow me to relate this personal story.

It is hard at times to know the best way to tell of personal encounters with the Lord. To many people, the mere suggestion of someone's saying, "The Lord spoke to me," is roughly equivalent to claiming they had tea that afternoon on the planet Venus with alien beings. To others, opinions about the relative validity of your report vary—from the notion you concocted the conversation yourself, to the cautious possibility that God just might have spoken.

To whatever category my testimony may relegate me in your judgment, I cannot describe one of my most important experiences in Christ without telling you it began with a specific set of words from Him. There were actually only three words—following which, neither the Lord nor I spoke. I did argue—debating mentally in my best forensic style as I recoiled from what He had spoken. Nevertheless, each argument was instantly deflated by so irrefutable a rebuttal that my debate was useless. It wasn't He who returned my argument. Simple honesty had me cornered. I simply and intuitively knew that to remain honest with

God's dealings in my own heart, I had to obey the command of that quiet, internal voice I recognized so well.

"Dance for me," the Voice said.

That's right. God told me to dance.

I had been at prayer for an extended period one morning, using the church sanctuary as my prayer room. No one was there, except for a few staff people in several of the offices. Thus, you can possibly appreciate my dilemma. Even if I did respond to the Voice and perform some holy jig—after all, who can say "No" to God—what were the chances it would remain between Him and me? What I felt I certainly didn't need was for someone to step in and witness the pastor cavorting about like a fanatic!

All the thoughts racing through my mind are difficult to summarize, as I futilely attempted to negotiate the situation with the Most High. I could instantly think of innumerable reasons for not dancing: it was *impractical, unnecessary, undesirable,* and entirely *unreasonable!* Yet none of the reasons was convincing, because deep down I knew the *real* issue. What God was dealing with was not dancing, but dignity—*false* dignity. It was raw, carnal, fear-filled, self-centered pride.

I was the victim of Michal's Syndrome—that common affliction that characterizes those of us who are more preoccupied with our style, sophistication, or dignity than we are with being childlike in praising God. Michal's Syndrome is subject to a wide variety of "expert" opinions. Like competing physicians trying to be first to identify a new virus, there are religious analysts who hasten to advance their varied opinions lest a contagion of simplicity rampage through the church. There is such a wide spectrum of opinions that if you simply, flatly *don't* want expressive worship, you can always find a spiritual expert whose "second opinion" will justify yours:

- "Well, some people just need a lot of exuberance. Others of us don't." (The implication is that *mature* people don't.)
- "It's all a matter of a person's cultural background. You and I are culturally reserved." (The implication is that "reserved" is socially superior or culturally advanced.)
- "You must watch out for emotionalism; it becomes *so* subjective and worship loses its objectivity in worshipping God and starts to center on man." (The theological concern for "God's glory" obviously makes this righteously unchallengeable.)
- "I believe—don't you?—that everyone should worship God in his own way, and according to his own beliefs. After all, to do otherwise is … well, it's … it's un-civil." You know, each of us should worship God according to the dictates of his own heart.
- (Smiling smugly) "I wouldn't let it worry me. After all, what difference can it make? God looks on the heart, anyway. All this activity doesn't add a thing!" (The ease with which the leader/counselor/observer dismisses it all as irrelevant consoles our quest for an escape from accountability as to our own responsiveness.)

The issue is expressiveness, openness, forthrightness—any assertive display of praise in worship settings beyond socially acceptable, cooperative singing. It begets a bevy of opinions from wild support to angered resistance. It has made me nervous many times, too.

Several of the above arguments had registered with me over the years. Having had a broad mixture of church background, running the gamut from Presbyterianism and Methodism to Pentecostalism, I knew the "do's" and "don'ts" of every circle in evangelical Christianity. When it came to acceptable and unacceptable worship practices, I knew dancing wasn't one that *any* of them approved. Therefore, I didn't like the idea at *all*, and felt that God Himself was bullying me to the wall on an issue we all had the right to differ over.

I had my theology to stand upon, too.

After all, I knew as I stood there—"Dance for me" still reverberating through my brain—that God's acceptance of me wasn't based on my antics at praise. I knew He doesn't measure anyone by a set of calisthenics! However, just as all these thoughts ran through my mind, I became aware of one stark fact: I could win this argument with *myself* but I would risk losing something with God. I recognized that my potential "loss" was a hard lesson in humility:

- in remaining as a child before the Father
- in keeping small in my own eyes
- in refusing the encrustation of religious sophistry that can inevitably calcify the bones of anyone's soul and grip them with a spiritual arthritis

Therefore, I danced.

I didn't do it well, but then, only God was looking. As I did, I felt within my heart the warm, contented witness that Abba Father was pleased.

I knew His pleasure wasn't because He had won an argument, but because I had won a victory. I knew He wasn't happy because He had managed to exploit my vulnerability, but because I had chosen to *remain* vulnerable. I knew He wasn't dangling me as a pawn-like toy because He needed my dancing, but because I needed to respond that way. He knew it was essential to ensure my future flexibility—my availability to learn the pathway of worship-unto-fruitfulness. The last point is so important—*fruitfulness*. Because the Michal Syndrome can lead anyone to a rationalized sense of superiority, it can come at the expense of a deadly, spiritual fruitlessness. Barrenness is a high price to pay for one's dignity.

That was one classic encounter with my own pride, of seeing "*my* majesty in the mirror," of coming to terms with the horrifying power of self-consciousness, fear, and pride to marshal their forces and plead successfully for their survival. However, seeing those liars parading as "my majesty," I determined to bow to *His* Majesty instead.

I share that testimony at my own expense and very much at the risk of sounding either disgustingly fanatical or impractically mystical. I relate it in order to help us hear more than my description of a moment's dance-of-death to pride. Rather, I invite our discussion of one of the biblical facts about worship and an issue that seems, inevitably, to become a battleground: expressiveness.

- bold, lively, joyous congregational singing
- spoken, spontaneous praises amid the congregation
- shouts of "Hallelujah!" or "Praise the Lord!"
- upraised hands stretched forth in worship
- clapping of hands, in tempo with the music or as an applause expressed to God

The list could lengthen, but the essence of the problem is on the table. We are at a great watershed of Christian worship and fellowship. There are strong opinions, deep emotions, and intense boundary lines drawn around this theme. To espouse an open, free response is to invite accusations: Confusion! Disorder! Charismatic! Emotionalism!

However, before conclusions or accusations of "silly" or "sectarian" practices increase, maybe it would be better to look into the Word of God. In doing so, David is a good point of reference, for in him we have a beautiful blend of (1) someone whose heart attitude is attested to by God and (2) someone whose *humility* was verified *before* God. With his combination of character and childlikeness, and with the evidence of the Word that flowed through his pen, we have a solid source of guidance in acceptable worship.

New Testament Worship

Peculiarly, David is a very *New* Testament place to begin. Though he lived a millennium before Christ, David's directives concerning worship in its form and practice influenced the worship traits of the first century, as the Old Testament was the only Bible they had.

Opponents of expressive worship occasionally accept that the New Testament does contain a few references to forthright, open praise. Still, the presumption is that expressiveness went out with the blood-sacrifice system, or that it was only a cultural trait of Hebrew tradition. It's as though enthusiastic or open praise went away at the same time as circumcision.

However, the essence of sacrifice has never left worship, and never will. "Therefore by Him let us continually offer the sacrifice of praise to God, that is, the fruit of *our* lips, giving thanks to His name" (Hebrews 13:15). As to writing off biblical expressiveness as an ancient cultural trait, we must wrestle with the question of God's Word and its authority to command our behavior regardless of our cultural environment. Any resistance I may naturally feel toward open, expressive worship is *not* justified on an appeal to my culture. The tendency of man has always been against the sacrifice of our own way and against surrender to His. Human nature's willfulness mandates that the Bible must remain the arbiter of my tastes, not my culture.

To begin, there are more direct references to expressive worship in the New Testament than usually meet the eye. Singing, praising, upraised voices, lifted hands, kneeling, offerings, and reading of the Scriptures are all mentioned.[1] Even though there are not many references, it does not eliminate the fact that New Testament worship was *full-spectrum.*

Every believer possesses the wisdom to recognize that worship is not a single-dimensional exercise of the human personality. It is certainly not a cerebral pursuit, a mystical consciousness, or an emotional binge; but it does involve reason, spiritual intuition, and emotions. According to the Scriptures, worship "in spirit and in truth" involves the total human being—*spirit, mind, emotions,* and *body.* Paul registered a clear-cut appeal for this order of worship. This paraphrase of Romans 12:1–2, with commentary, underscores the multidimensional nature of New Testament worship, and the requirement it makes to go *beyond* mere human reasoning and to *enter* in and participate:

> *"Therefore I appeal to you, brothers* [an emotional call based on all the revelation preceding in chapters 1–11], *as you witnessed and experienced God's mercies* [a further expression reaching to touch the heart], *that you bring before Him a sacrifice of worship fully alive at every dimension—involving your body* [physical], *your mind* [intellectual], *and your spirit* [spiritual]. *This is wholly acceptable as a sacrifice and is the most intelligent and spiritual worship possible. To achieve this, you must break free of the world-mind and allow the Spirit to transform your thinking in*

*order that you may discover the full counsel of God's
will"* (Romans 12:1–2 author's paraphrase, emphasis
added).[2]

The New Testament worshipper, of course, has gone beyond
the era of *blood* sacrifice, for there is no longer *any* requirement
of sacrifices for sin. Christ has fulfilled those requirements as
our Savior, the Lamb of God. However, David foresaw our day
and described the timeless spirit of sacrifice that would forever
be essential when worship is offered to the Living God: "For You
do not desire sacrifice, or else I would give *it*; You do not delight
in burnt offering. The sacrifices of God *are* a broken spirit, a
broken and a contrite heart—These, O God, You will not
despise" (Psalm 51:16–17).

Such sacrifices *are* physical and they *do* require humility. The
basic meaning of *proskuneo*, the New Testament Greek word
for worship, corresponds to *shawkhaw*, the Old Testament
Hebrew term. Both mean *to prostrate oneself*. As physical as that
terminology is, and as possible as it actually is to do in private
devotion, the possibility of lying face down is neither practical,
required, nor generally recommended when believers gather in
assembly. Nevertheless, there is a prostrating that ought *always*
to be required—the prostrating of pride and the flattening
of the human will, which so readily inclines to assert its own
dignity at the expense of humble participation in full-hearted,
spiritually alive, and physically expressed worship.

Body Language

Michal's objection was to David's physical expressiveness in
worship. He might have marched sedately, sung discreetly, or

thought noble thoughts interminably, but the sparks flew when he danced.

They still do.

People still become upset when physical or verbal expressiveness exceeds their learned limits, and one can find in the Scriptures excess or tastelessness that cannot be rationalized. However, the irony of our reaction to excess is that we race to the other extreme. If someone shrieks aloud in a fanatical (possibly demonic) display, grossly interrupting a service where new expressiveness is being attempted, the likelihood is that the counter-move will be a virtual full retreat—a return to cold reserve and the safety of relative silence—and not just now, but *from now on*. The dummies and the demons win. The sincere are silenced as it seems our only perceived security against fanatical intrusion or noisy extremism is an equally ridiculous *nothing*.

So it is that *verbal praising* has become taboo in some circles, and understandably so, given the bizarre cases of (the never-actually-seen, but "we've heard that") oft-reported stereotypes that spook people from trying. The same goes for upraised hands or clapping. It only takes one or two people in a group who flail their arms mindlessly during any or every song, or who become "clap-happy" at the drop of any phrase from the pulpit. The few constitute a threat of stupid display that can reduce an entire congregation to an absolute unwillingness to attempt what otherwise are very biblical expressions of praise and worship.

It would be best to leave this dilemma alone if it weren't for the fact that the issue touches at the core of my point. You see, it is precisely at *this* point, open public expressiveness, that our will to humble ourselves is most delicately touched. The inclination to preserve my dignity or to reserve "my right to not participate" is confronted by such directives in the Word as this: "Oh, clap your hands, all you peoples! Shout to God with the voice of triumph! For the Lord Most High *is* awesome; *He is* a great King over all the earth" (Psalm 47:1–2). However, people still find sufficient reasons to justify excuses for not responding to God's Word when it exhorts: Clap! Shout!

There is an inescapable sanity to the "body language" of applause at appropriate points in worship that many fail to acknowledge. The command calls for such praise based on our Lord's triumphant victory. This should overcome any reservation we might have on the supposition that such expressiveness is superficial. Have you ever heard someone say, "I think that people who applaud in church are not regarding God with sufficient reverence"? It may be true, they are not, but even if that were so, their shallowness does not justify my indifference to the biblical command. I'm capable of employing an eerie kind of pride that excuses me from responsiveness because I feel someone else may be responding without the depth of understanding I feel that I have. I can only nurse such false reasoning if I am willing to violate two other commands: (1) *Not* to judge others whose hearts I cannot see, and (2) *to* present my *body* as a forthright worshipper.

The Scriptures call us to glorify God with high praises when you and I gather with the Church:

> Let them exalt Him also in the assembly of the people (Psalm 47:1–2).

> I will give You thanks in the great assembly; I will praise You among many people (Psalm 35:18).

> Shout joyfully to the Lord, all the earth: break forth in song, rejoice, and sing praises (Psalm 98:4).

Of course, "noise" isn't the object. Mere noisiness is never a virtue. It is unfortunate, however, that reverence has come to be equated with silence, or at least as a reserved quietness. To the contrary, there are some situations in which the *least* appropriate response is a reserved silence. The celebration of God's loving-kindness, the manifestation of His power, the testimony of His faithfulness—all may inspire praiseful expressiveness. "Blessed *are* the people who know the joyful sound! They walk, O Lord, in the light of Your countenance [face]" (Psalm 89:15). That "joyful sound" may be applause, laughter, praise, or triumphant song, but it can only sound forth from a liberated, sensitive worshipper. David's example urges us toward being both. It is possible to experience the release of that joy when discreet leadership and a responsive congregation join heart and hands to do so with balance and beauty.

The Congregation as a Choir

It is the uniting of a congregation—an assembled *body* of worshippers—that allows for the most beautiful and dynamic *body language*. A confidence and freedom comes when a group has moved beyond being just a miscellaneous assortment of worshippers to a cohesive, worshipful body. As long as expressiveness is merely tolerated and widely scattered, participation will always remain sporadic—at the whim of any individual worshipper—and real freedom will not come to a congregation. The quest for both liberty and unity requires that the leadership teach, define, and direct. This begins by distinguishing between *individuality* and *spontaneity*. *"Individuality"* can be whimsical, disordered, or counterproductive because it prevents real unity in congregational worship. However, spontaneity isn't whimsical—it's responsive. A whole congregation can participate *together in* spontaneous responsiveness.

Let me elaborate.

Because there are so many verses in the Bible showing more expressiveness than we generally practice, an honesty with Scripture brings hunger to many earnest worshippers who inquire, "How can we do this?" Their "How?" is not so much a question of form as it is, "How can this be done in a decent and orderly way?" Of course, that's also a scriptural concern, for all things *are* to be done that way. (The Greek text is more literally rendered "in a gracious and charming way" (1 Corinthians 14:40)). How can such specific practices as upraised hands, clapping, or concerted verbal praise be "in order," or for that matter, "decent"?

Having led worship and observed it among many different traditions, I believe that what confounds the possibility of fullest release are false ideas about the supposed righteousness of *individuality*—anyone doing *anything* at *any time* they feel like it. For some, their complete independence is their sole definition of liberty. For them, submission to headship means surrender to manipulation, and agreed cooperation with a *whole* congregation is a sacrifice of their liberty. However, honesty with experience reveals that when such a spirit prevails, the only "free" person in the worship service will be the one "*taking* their liberty." The rest of the assembly become "bound"—*bound* to endure whatever the "liberated" member does, because his "individuality" holds them at his mercy.

Because I longed to see our congregation move toward unity in an expressive, childlike, humble, and spiritually sensitive approach to worship, I knew we would have to deal with historic false notions about individuality. To circumvent that "takeover" spirit of "do-my-own-thing-ism," which is nothing more than a tyrannical lack of consideration of others, I introduced the concept of "the congregation as a choir."

It doesn't take a great mind to understand that a choir could never function in either beauty or worshipfulness if its members operated independently of one another. People can easily see the incongruity of a choir functioning in any other way than *together*. If we demonstrate illustrations of the point, it can provide for considerable humor and greatly strengthen the point!

That *togetherness* was at the heart of the apostle Paul's appeal to the congregation in Corinth: "Brethren, *when you come together* ...." His whole purpose in 1 Corinthians 14 is not to remove liberty, but to call for it by teaching people the idea of order—orchestration in worship without a suffocation in spirit. He directed them to an order that removed the confusion that had evolved from unwise, impulsive practices by individuals in the assembly. Their sincerity wasn't in question, but the relative wisdom of such independent behavior was.

The agreement of a congregation to move together as a choir, under the direction of their worship leader or pastor, is not a surrender to manipulation or mindless participation. It is an entry into unity, and an entry into a genuine liberty that becomes dynamic as sincere worshippers participate together in praise, in song, in upraised hands, in applause, or in a concerted shout—"Hallelujah!"

The Path of Praise

It was David who taught Israel to worship at new levels—from new songs to new instruments to new demonstrations of praise. There is something about David's leading the people to a new Tabernacle that has deep meaning for us today. In Acts 15, when the early Church's leaders gathered in council to determine to what degree Gentile converts would be required to maintain Old Testament ordinances, James addressed the situation with a quotation from the Prophet Amos:

> After this I will return and will rebuild the tabernacle of David, which has fallen down; I will rebuild its ruins, and I will set it up; So that the rest of mankind may seek the Lord, Even all the Gentiles who are called by My name, Says the Lord who does all these things (Acts 15:16–17).

James' insight applied this passage to help solve the question they faced then, but interestingly enough, that same passage has another application for us today. James' focus was on "*all the Gentiles [nations]*" flowing together to the worship of God. Our focus is on *the worship itself*. It excites the imagination of those who can see that this prophecy of God's last-days gathering of the nations includes a prophecy of a last-days rebuilding of the Tabernacle of David!

David's Tabernacle was, in his time, more than a renewal—it was a reformation. There was an adjustment forward and a newness everywhere. Prevailing above it all was a humble, childlike spirit of praise that paved the path to fruitfulness, joy, and victory. David's expressiveness was at the heart of this breakthrough, just as Michal's resistance was at its throat. However, as surely as we may avoid Michal's Syndrome and its consequent barrenness, we can enter into the new reformation. A willingness to accept David's heart attitude *and* childlike exuberance in praise may bring us to a *local "rebuilding"* of David's Tabernacle. It holds such high promise of real rejoicing and abounding fruit. It is worth moving toward the formation of a congregation that learns to worship as a choir; singing unto the Lord a new song, praising in unity, and humbly coming into God's presence with free expressiveness and thanksgiving.

The reward of worship is God's enthroned presence.

David sang, "But You are holy, Enthroned in the praises of Israel". This oft-quoted statement from Psalm 22:3 deserves our greatest understanding, since the implications of the verb *yawshab* are dramatic. Though the basic idea of the word is "to sit down," when the King of the Universe is the subject, it is appropriately translated "enthroned." David resounds this great truth to every generation: *Praise creates a dwelling place for God in man's present situation!*

He is not saying that praise makes God bigger or more powerful: Nonsense! Nor is he saying that praise forces God to take any particular action: He is Sovereign! However, the text *does* say that when you praise God—whatever the situation—you can count on Him moving into the middle of it! Thus, it is understandable why a worshipping, praising congregation is so desirable an entity:

- It is desirable to God, who is seeking those who will worship Him in spirit and in truth.
- It is fulfilling to those who worship, for God visits them in blessing and in power.
- It is desirable for those who enter into such a setting, even though they may be new to it.

People will recognize God's presence and they will respond to it, since there are few human beings who do not deeply, honestly hunger for vital touch with the fountain of their being.

My deep desire for the continued prospect of His presence is what prompted me to remind our congregation of the strong promptings to praise we have received as the Holy Spirit of exhortation has operated among us (1 Corinthians 14:1–5). I wrote:

> That praise has been a hallmark of our corporate life is well known, and that it is a generally accepted practice in our midst is very clear. However, that praise must remain eminent in our understanding and participation is the point of this review. Over the years, some lovely truths have been welded together as the Spirit has brought edification and comfort. Here is the gist of some basic messages that He has delivered to us:

> 1. The *darkness surrounds* this hour as it did Paul and Silas in the Philippian prison. Their praise brought God's hand by an earthquake and out of the night, a hopeless jailer was saved. Now, let your praises rise. As you praise continually, *spiritual shock waves* go out into the world around you. It will bring your release and the release of many into the Kingdom of God (Acts 16:19–34).
> 2. *Praise* is *your pathway* through the mired circumstances of the present world. Your step will be uncertain and slide unless you recognize that your *praises form stepping-stones* by which the Father paves your way into the future purpose He has for you (Psalm 26).
> 3. Praise the Lord. Sing unto the Lord. Sing with your spirit and sing with your understanding, for as *you sing praises' unto Him, He continues* His great creative working ... and in your midst you shall see the marvelous works of God, the Lord of the *new* creation (Job 38:4–7).

I once heard someone say, "'Let's just praise the Lord' is a rather closed view of things." I understood their meaning, for they had come from a circle of folks who neither praised the Lord "with understanding," as the psalmist commands, nor did they have a corporate *forward march* mentality—as David and his people manifested. One must agree that praise-for-praise's sake can become a weary and pointless experience.

However, there is a path of praise that leads to life, and many are moving forward on it with great joy, growth, and renewal. David walked that path and, in childlike abandon, broke into leaping and dancing. His humility of heart brought a ready response to the Holy Spirit of joy motivating him, and—even though Michal protested—David's Tabernacle was built, it housed the Ark, and it was filled with the praises of the Lord.

I vote to help build it again!

11

The Life-Begetting Power of Song

"Sing, O barren, you *who* have not borne!
Break forth into singing ... for you shall
expand to the right and to the left, And
your descendants will inherit the nations."
Isaiah 54:1–3

SHE WAS THE picture of shyness, standing at the door bashfully glancing my way, with one finger curled to her lower lip and her eyes eloquently inquiring, "Can I see you, Pastor Jack?"

I beckoned to her, and the eight-year-old walked across the prayer room to where I stood with some elders. Though the service was about to begin, I knelt to greet the child so our eyes were at the same level:

"Hi, Aimee." I smiled. "What do you want?"

She was so sweetly childlike. "Pastor Jack, I wanted you to hear a song the Lord gave to me."

The service was imminent, but right then she seemed a more precious and urgent matter than the multitude gathering for worship.

"Sing it for me," I said. She did.

It was a tender little tune. The child's loving lyric voiced her worship, and gave expression to first discoveries in the Holy Spirit's creativity in song.

"That's beautiful, Aimee. You keep singing it to the Lord Jesus, will you?"

She nodded and we hugged each other as I whispered, "Thank you for coming to share your song with me. Tell Mama and Daddy hello for me, and ... ," I paused and then added, "I love you."

Her smile would have melted a million hearts as she said, "I love you too," then slipped out the door and hurried to sit with her mom and dad.

There's more to Aimee's story, but for the moment, I pause to underscore a conviction about worship and song: God *wants to give everyone their own song of praise to Him.*

The Creator, whose Word repeatedly says, "Sing unto the Lord a new song," wants to birth a new song on the lips and from the hearts of His own—a distinctly new song of your own! I'm not suggesting, however, that everyone's new song is appropriate for everybody or that these songs should supplant ones we've learned together.

However, my response to Aimee's song was more than a pastor's kindness to a child; it was my confirmation of a vital practice. She had never heard me encourage private song-making in worship, but at her tender age, she was experiencing a creative possibility open to us all.[1]

The Full Spectrum of Song

Worship may be possible without song, but nothing contributes more to its beauty, majesty, dignity, or nobility, nor to its tenderness and intimacy. There is a full spectrum of purposes and practices of song in worship. The breadth of styles, the endless melodic possibilities, the delicate nuances of choral dynamics, the brilliant luster of instrumental arrangement, the soul-stirring anthems of anointed choirs, the rumbling magnificence of giant organs—all seem clearly to be a God-given means for our endless expression in worship. New musical expression is fitting as we each discover new things about the manifold wisdom of the Lord our God.

God's Word is full of the music of worship from creation to Revelation and—while songs of praise existed long before his time—it's to David we usually turn to learn songs from the Scriptures. He seems to have cultivated its use to a dimension previously unexplored.

After raising the Tabernacle in Jerusalem and anticipating the building of the Temple, David organized and provided for the support of music leaders and ministries to enhance Israel's worship. Choirs and orchestras not only were prepared to sing and play skillfully, they were also selected for their sensitivity to the spirit of prophecy. The careful detail in the listing of specific duties of those who served (1 Chronicles 25:1–5) tells us something of the importance given to music under David's rule:

- All these *were* under the direction of their father for the music *in* the house of the Lord
- [they] prophesied according to the order of the king
- [they were] to give thanks and to praise the Lord
- [being] instructed in the song of the Lord

This description reveals a blend both of spontaneity to the Holy Spirit and preparedness for skilled musical presentation. Their prophesying involved more than setting existing Scripture to music. These musicians were to wait on the Lord for inspiration—for living truth that would ignite worship and joy in the hearts of God's people. Nevertheless, they did not neglect duty in the name of mysticism. They learned the Lord's song in two ways: (1) in their work on instruments and voice, and (2) in their waiting on the Spirit of God.

David's era provides insights beyond the obvious value of organizing church music leadership. It issues a summons to awakening and advancement. Since Moses longed for the day that all of God's people would "prophesy" (Numbers 11:29), shouldn't we also expect choirs and instruments to minister with the Holy Spirit's gift of prophecy? Is it possible that the New Testament "restoration of the Tabernacle of David" will bring us to new dimensions of Holy Spirit-inspired praise and worship in song? There is a lovely balance in David's institution of musically skilled and spiritually anointed worship. His blend of order and flexibility is hard to attain in any era, but his approach deserves a fresh welcome in today's Church.

What guidelines does the New Testament offer us for expecting and cultivating music in corporate and personal worship? It is extremely significant that two epistles issue explicit directives to sing "psalms, hymns, and spiritual songs." The apostle Paul explains that the purpose is more than belting out religious tunes, odes, and ditties. Both epistles relate song to spiritual growth: "Let the word of Christ dwell in you richly ... singing" (Colossians 3:15–16), "And do not be drunk with wine ... but be filled with the Spirit ... singing" (Ephesians 5:18–19). The first establishes a direct relationship between the Word and worship, while the second calls for the Spirit in worship.

A closer look at these verses not only establishes the value of music in New Testament worship, but also opens a new area in worship—something we might expect under the new covenant:

> Let the word of Christ dwell in you richly in all
> wisdom, teaching and admonishing one another in
> psalms and hymns and spiritual songs, singing with
> grace in your hearts to the Lord (Colossians 3:16).

Here, the writer links the fruitful implanting of the Word of God to our singing and worshipping. Most of us would think of these as separate operations—the Word as instructional and song as inspirational. Instead, human intellect and emotion are integrated *through* song, and effective teaching is said to require worship for its fullest accomplishment. The complement of worshipful song helps us assimilate the meat of the Word into our character and conduct. Just as our digestive systems process food and distribute nutrients throughout the body, so worshipful singing is apparently essential for the integration of the Word into our life.

Could the music of worship be the means God has ordained for fulfilling the covenant made long ago?

> But this *is* the covenant that I will make ... I will put
> My law in their minds, and write it on their hearts
> (Jeremiah 31:33).

> I will put My Spirit within you and cause you to walk
> in My statutes, and you will keep My judgments and
> do *them* (Ezekiel 36:27).

Perhaps it's true that Holy Spirit-filled worship is the distinct means by which the new covenant transcends the old in terms of the "*Word*-in-our-lives." No longer is the Word engraved on stone or confined to parchment, but its precepts are being infused into the human personality. Recognizing the place of song in this process certainly reveals the priority of worship. Our singing becomes infinitely more than droning out another ode to orthodoxy. Worshipful singing expedites a process that quickens our minds to receive the Word and submits our souls to the Holy Spirit's implanting it within us. Spirit-filled worship may be our insurance against merely learning facts from the Bible instead of receiving power through its teaching.

In this light, Paul's second mention of singing becomes all the more meaningful. Two direct commands stand in stark juxtaposition: *"Don't* be unwise. *Do know* God's will!" Then follows the call to sing:

> Don't be drunk with wine, it only dissipates you;
> rather, keep on being refilled with the Holy Spirit,
> a path practiced best by continued singing among
> yourselves of psalms, hymns, and spiritual songs
> (Ephesians 5:18–19 author's paraphrase).

There is no mystery to the message here: if you want to walk in God's will and wisdom, avoid the world's spirit and keep filled with God's Spirit. Song-filled worship is the way to do both!

This destroys any notion that music is extracurricular. It is essential to growth, wisdom, understanding, and godly fruitfulness. Word-centeredness joins Spirit-fullness at the altar of songful worship. This balance confronts anyone's temptation to sacrifice either, since both are interdependent.

So clear an assignment and such potential fruit mandate our familiarity with "psalms, hymns, and spiritual songs." What are they and how can we apply them in worship?

Singing Psalms

The New Testament Church—Jew and Gentile alike—accepted and used the worship literature of the Old Testament. The

Church viewed Scripture as God's inspired Word, and worship from this source was foremost. Singing "psalms" was not only to sing the *words* of the text, but also to sing the inspired utterances of God! Singing psalms was God-glorifying and life-instilling because God's Word was being breathed into the heart as it was breathed out in song.

Today's psalm singing is mostly songs comprised of Scripture. The new reformation has sparked more singing of God's Word in the last twenty years than perhaps any time in Church history. Yet while this has been happening, we occasionally see a strange, fearful questioning or resistance to this development.

A pastor friend who had just accepted a new pastorate related the anger of some of his congregation when he introduced Scripture songs. He hadn't replaced any of the music the people were familiar with, but was only offering some new songs with biblical lyrics. On occasion, he had asked the people to sing directly from their Bibles as he taught the lovely new melodies, thinking they would appreciate being able to carry God's Word in their hearts through song. Not so.

"We won't sing it if it isn't in the hymnal!" some spouted. It was incredible!

Tragically, their clinging to tradition had so warped their viewpoint on worship that they didn't realize (1) they were being led by a faithful shepherd to do exactly what the Bible says, and (2) however unwittingly, they were scorning God's own Word by their resistance. Peculiarly, they exalted a hymnal of brilliant but merely *human* inspiration, above the eternal Word of *divine* inspiration.

I happen to know that particular pastor. Without question, he was being sensitive in attempting new music with his congregation. However, some of us may appreciate guidelines when teaching *any* new forms of worship. These have proved helpful:

1. *Give a biblical basis for what you introduce.* Show the idea in the Word itself, and show its practical benefits, too. People usually respond to truth when they see it, especially when seeing the potential promises within those teachings.

2. *Don't try to accomplish too much, too fast.* The Bible likens people to sheep—not horses or cattle. Lead them slowly. Stampeding or rushing them creates unrest, and will likely bring failure.

3. *Never propose something new as an opponent of something old.* When introducing new music, worship forms, or songs, pushiness or arrogance about either the old or the new will never come across favorably. Lead into the new from a positive base of love rather than a negative base of criticism toward the old.

Singing Hymns

Our word *hymn* is derived from the Greek *humnois,* which was simply the word for a religious song. Every generation writes its own songs *about* the Lord and *to* Him. Whether in the first or twenty-first century, hymns are songs of testimony, triumph, exaltation, adoration, and celebration.

I was first taught that hymns were (1) great doctrinal statements set to music, or (2) declarations of objective praise to God. I later learned a broader definition that was more appropriate. Hymns span a wide range of music—wider than some of us might like. For my part, I would prefer "Immortal, Invisible, God Only Wise" to "I'll Fly Away, O Glory," and "Blessed Assurance" to "Little Brown Church in the Vale." Nonetheless, an honest definition derived from the New Testament word requires latitude beyond individual tastes.

The distinct requirement of a Christian hymn is not its caliber or quality, but its subject matter. Technically, "hymn" refers to the lyrics while "melody" or "tune" to the song. However, whether sung or spoken, the subject is *God*—His grace, His works, His purpose, His people, His power, His glory, or His Person. I don't recall being told this, but I apparently caught the basic idea of "hymns" early in life, when I thought of them as "*HIMs*—Songs about the Lord!"

In some renewal congregations, the more classic, traditional hymns have suffered disuse of late—hymnals often being discarded as irrelevant, musty artifacts of an unrenewed era. But as surely as people become what they eat, a congregation becomes what they sing, and there is something sturdy, durable, and anchor-like about the hymns born of earlier renewals. We need them fused into our souls along with the newer songs in vogue today.

Older hymns sometimes "die" in church because of the way they're sung. A remedy? *Don't* drag *them!* There is nothing reverent about *slow*. Some people reject hymns simply because they are bored by them, but you can keep interest alive. Brisk and bright is better than dumpy and dead. I'm not appealing for jackrabbit jive or racehorse rhythms, but turtle-like tempos need to be sent out to sea forever!

Singing Spiritual Songs

There are wide differences in definitions of "spiritual songs," and I don't want to appear either ignorant or critical of any of them. However, I want to discuss my opinion that "spiritual songs" were the apostle Paul's reference to a distinct music form unique to the Church. It was one that would help fulfill the prospect of God wanting to give everyone their own song of praise to Him.

Spiritual songs have been defined as informal choruses, choral anthems, simpler, more personal statements of faith or brief, less complex odes of worship. But I propose that they were a new music form unavailable until the New Testament—until Christ's full redemption allowed the Holy Spirit to dwell in mankind. Clearly, early believers sang "spiritual songs" of worship; what were they?

Hodais pneumatikais, the exact words in both Ephesians 5 and Colossians 3, is usually translated "spiritual songs."[2] The first word is simply "ode," the Greek term for any words that were sung. However, the second word—*pneumatikais*—seems to be the key to the full meaning of this phrase.

Pneumatikais—an obvious cognate to *pneuma* (spirit)—is most easily defined and understood noting its use elsewhere in the New Testament. For example, Paul uses this word when introducing the subject of spiritual gifts in 1 Corinthians 12:1 (literally *pneumatika*—"spiritual things"). Later in his appeal to the Galatians concerning their duty to restore fallen brethren, the word also appears: "You who are spiritual ones ... " (*pneumatikoi*) are assigned the task of that restoring ministry. Although *pneumatic* occurs over twenty times in the New Testament, these two texts give us something of a basic picture. *Pneumatika* seems to indicate Holy Spirit-filled people of character and charisma.

Their *character* is noted in the Galatian text, "you who are *spiritual ones* restore the fallen ... " (Galatians 6:1 author's paraphrase). Their *charisma* (in the sense of their functioning in the charismatic gifts of the Holy Spirit) is indicated in their apparent acceptance and response to "spiritual things," i.e., manifestations of the Holy Spirit's gifts (1 Corinthians 12:7).

These factors alone would not finalize a definition, except for the fact that in this same context Paul discusses "singing with the spirit and with the understanding." It is here in 1 Corinthians 12–14, as the apostle corrects their abuse of glossolalia, that he discusses singing of a distinctly Holy Spirit-enabled nature.

> For if I pray in a tongue, my spirit prays, but my understanding is unfruitful. What is *the conclusion* then? I will pray with the spirit, and I will also pray with the understanding. I will sing with the spirit, and I will also sing with the understanding (1 Corinthians 14:14–15).

His distinguishing singing "with the spirit" from "singing with the understanding" points to what "spiritual songs" may have meant in the first-century church; an exercise separate from, yet complementary to, the singing of psalms and hymns.

Since the general passage beginning in 1 Corinthians 12:1 and the specific text beginning in 1 Corinthians 14:1 *both* use *pneumatika* to describe the kind of subject matter being dealt with, it follows that the distinct type of singing referred to as being "with the spirit (*pneuma*)" could be the same as "spiritual songs." I would not be so stubborn as to oppose another interpretation, but I propose that the whole of the New Testament context supports the definition of "spiritual songs" as being Holy Spirit-enabled utterances that:

- were sung rather than spoken
- were most commonly to be a part of one's devotional life
- were explained or interpreted if exercised in corporate gatherings and
- were so desirable as to have Paul assert his personal "will" to practice them—"I *will* sing with the spirit" (1 Corinthians 14:15).

I would not preclude the possibility or desirability of spiritual songs being in the native language of the worshipper nor suggest that one (glossolalia or native tongue) was preferable to another. However, it does seem clear that the Holy Spirit is at work in this worship expression, doing something distinctly valid and valuable.

We can understand the practicality of this exercise when we remind ourselves how God has given the gift of worship for our edification as well as for His exaltation. It shouldn't surprise us if the gift of song for worship, praise, thanksgiving, and adoration should provide one of its three forms in an arena of free, completely original, personal expression. Such spontaneity in personal worship may allow me the liberty of lyricizing my own heart's joy or pain, lifting it with a melody I spontaneously breathe forth. To sing this way removes the restrictions of poetic rhyme and meter or musical rhythm and form. A practical, scriptural, and desirable thing occurs. A previously unsung song—a *new song*—comes forth from worshipping lips, adoring Him and releasing the soul to broader dimensions of glorifying the Creator.

Thus, the spiritual song rounds out a triad of music forms given to the Church:

1. In *psalms*, we declare His *Word* in song; we learn and rehearse the eternal, unchanging Word of His revealed truth in the Scriptures.
2. In *hymns*, we announce His *works* in song; we praise Him and review His attributes, testifying to His goodness as experienced over the centuries.
3. In *spiritual songs*, we welcome His *will* in song; we give place to the Holy Spirit's refilling, and make place for His Word to "dwell richly" within.[3]

Re-Choiring the Church

With such a wide variety of musical means, with music so universally enjoyed, and with so unsurpassed an avenue for expressing human thought and emotion, why is the Church's music so often the focal point of such problems or difficulty? Why is it so hard to get the people to learn new hymns, to sing joyously, to respond with spontaneity, or to accept new music forms? Why is the choir too loud or too soft, too hard to understand, too ineffective, or too overpowering? Why is the minister of music, the choral director, or the organist "too demanding," "so undependable," "such a prima donna," "given to favoritism," and so on?

One thing that did more to expand our own horizons in corporate worship came about through repeated frustration and failure. We couldn't get a choir to last.

I love choral music very much. I not only enjoy hearing choirs, but also singing in them. Since my first experience in leading a music group when I was six years old, I have helped form and lead choirs for everything from radio broadcasts to college tours—not to mention *church*. Yet, despite my best efforts, every early attempt in our pastorate in Van Nuys met with dismal results—no choir.

Each new try involved capable people. Each beginning seemed exciting for everyone. However, after three tries in as many years, I began to draw the conclusion that God was trying to tell me something. I surrendered the idea that we needed a choir to the Lord. I don't suggest that what happened to us is everyone's answer. Nevertheless, there is no question that God's declared moratorium on our efforts to form a choir became the key to unleashing the song of our congregation, for I asked the whole congregation to be our choir. I've already related the way this tactic has allowed a freedom without foolishness, but here's how it all began.

I began to treat the church the way I would a choir. I started one Sunday by describing the conclusion that I had reached following the above failures at choir formation. I didn't believe the vision for a congregation-wide choir was more spiritual than otherwise. I didn't feel choirs were an unholy tradition that we should abandon, but rather that we were all to be "the choir" for the present season in our body life. (Incidentally, we *still* treat the body as a choir, but we also have six vocal and two handbell choirs.)

I did three things to help apply this concept.

First, I taught from the Word of God. The Book of Revelation unveils a massive angelic choir of worshippers in heaven. "And the number of them was ten thousand times ten thousand, and thousands of thousands" (Revelation 5:11). The Book of Hebrews goes even further, and amazingly puts us *all* in that heavenly choir, there at God's Throne, sounding our praises beside the angelic choir, and joining in the timeless worship of the Most High.

> But you have come to Mount Zion and to the city of the living God, the heavenly Jerusalem, to an innumerable company of angels (Hebrews 12:22).

As these and other truths of the Word began to register, something came unshackled! Suddenly the congregation perceived themselves in a new light—joined to the heavenly angel choir! Biblical truth had set them free to worship with a new sense of privilege and responsibility. I sometimes wonder if, more than we know, the presence of a good choir at times becomes an unintended substitute for a congregation's commitment to minister to the Lord. Our absence of a formed choir became a pivotal point for releasing everyone to be the choir.

Second, even today I often address the congregation as a choir. For example: "Good morning! As we begin worship today, will the entire choir stand with me, and …" My gesture clearly encompasses the whole body and smiles come over their faces. Everyone knows what I mean, but if I see a bewildered visitor, I add, "At The Church On The Way we've decided that the whole congregation will constitute the choir, so if you're visiting us today, join right in. We're not an exclusive group; in fact, some of us have terrible voices, but boy do we sing! Join in like you've been here a hundred years, and no one will know the difference."

Third, this approach has done wonders in solving one of any congregation's most challenging problems: how to get the people to learn new music, songs, and hymns.

Most people are hesitant to attempt new songs. I guess we all have a residual fear of appearing foolish. Consequently, new songs are tough to introduce because the price of learning new music seems high. It seems to take so long—going over and over a song. Moreover, the service's movement suffers, especially if the song is ineptly taught or inappropriately introduced.

However, once the congregation perceives itself as the choir, a subtle but significant change occurs in the people's mindset. To introduce a new hymn or worship chorus, I'll say, "Choir, we're going to rehearse a new song. Don't worry about making mistakes—we're all learning it together. There's just one requirement: if you make a mistake, make a loud one." People laugh, the atmosphere is relaxed, and with fear removed the learning process is speedy, fulfilling, and quite frankly, *fun*. Such a "re-choiring" of the Body of Christ opens the way to spiritual advance. The corporate gathering is released into praise and worship, and each individual believer begins to view himself more seriously as a genuine "Minister to the Lord."

The Sheer Power of Song

There are places in the Bible that the sheer power of song explodes upon our understanding. I mean far more than the power of song to express joy, rejoicing, praiseful thanks, or unified worship. I'm talking about song as an instrument of miracles—of power works. I'm talking about instances in which the Bible shows songs becoming power-filled for *battle*, for *breakthrough*, and for *birthing*.

The Song of Battle

The story of Judea's King Jehoshaphat and his victory over the invasion staged by the combined troops of Moab and Ammon is a great argument against the idea that history is boring.

Vastly outnumbered by an alien host bent on their extermination, he and his people made the Lord their first point of resort. With prayer and fasting, they turned to God, rather than appealing to a neighboring nation as a hired gun to come and rescue them. God answered their call:

> Listen, all you of Judah and you inhabitants of
> Jerusalem, and you, King Jehoshaphat! Thus says the
> Lord to you: "Do not be afraid nor dismayed because
> of this great multitude, for the battle *is* not yours,
> but God's. ... You will not *need* to fight in this *battle*.
> Position yourselves, stand still and see the salvation of
> the Lord, who is with you, O Judah and Jerusalem!" Do
> not fear or be dismayed; tomorrow go out against them,
> for the Lord *is* with you (2 Chronicles 20:15–17).

Jehoshaphat and the people responded with awe and praise, but what makes this event memorable—and unique in the annals of military encounters—is the strategy they employed in battle.

They took a peculiar action based on the raw conviction that God meant what He said: "You will not need to fight in this battle."

The choir preceded the army and the singers preceded the warriors.

Nobody dictated this arrangement. They just concluded this battle was different. Here's how it happened:

> So they rose early in the morning ... and as they
> went out, Jehoshaphat stood and said, "Hear me,
> O Judah and you inhabitants of Jerusalem: Believe
> in the Lord your God, and you shall be established;
> believe His prophets, and you shall prosper." And
> when he had consulted with the people, he appointed
> those who should sing ... and who should praise the
> beauty of holiness, as they went out before the army
> and were saying: "Praise the Lord, For His mercy
> *endures* forever." Now when they began to sing and
> to praise, the Lord set ambushes against the people
> of Ammon, Moab, and Mount Seir ... and they
> were defeated ... they helped to destroy one another
> (2 Chronicles 20:20–23).

God's people lifted their song of praise and expressed their belief in His promise. When they did, their enemies were so confounded by it all they turned on one another!

It's a great story, but is it relevant today? Although some people are nervous about taking Old Testament events and applying the principles of faith they provide to today's circumstances, I think there's truth here for us now. Let me illustrate.

Wyn Lewis is Pastor of London's Kensington Temple, just down the road from Prince Charles and Lady Diana's city dwelling at Kensington Palace. He recently told me of a demanding season of spiritual struggle he and his congregation experienced some years ago.

An exceptional time of evangelism had brought burgeoning growth, but it had also attracted the attention of a band of spiritists in that part of London. An entire coven of witches had begun attempting an infiltration of the services at the Temple.

Anyone who knows the concentrated power of evil when demonic powers are focused against a holy enterprise can appreciate the invisible warfare that begins to ignite in such a setting. Wyn told me:

> One evening, as I rose to preach, the oppression in the sanctuary was so strong I knew I must do something before beginning my message.
>
> The building was full, mostly with Christians committed to Christ's testimony. I said, "Brethren and sisters, I think you sense that we are facing a spiritual battle. You and I know that our strength is simply to lift up praise—to sing the overcoming song of our Lord Jesus' victory in the Cross."
>
> I began to lead the people, singing one song after another about the Blood of Jesus, knowing that the Bible teaches that hell is routed when believers exalt the blood of the Lamb at the heart of their testimony (Revelation 12:11).
>
> As we were singing, suddenly, those who had been assigned to bind in an unholy agreement against God's free and powerful workings in that place, began to rise and run from the room—hands over their ears against the praises of the saints. Needless to say, it was a night of great victory and salvation, and it ended that particular season of spiritual skirmish.

The song of the Lord is a mighty instrument for spiritual battle. The Lord would call us to worship Him with song when faced with an enemy that is too strong for us. We can see our song become a musical power play and find victory in our circumstances as we obey the directive to worship with song. It's a timeless resource that God's Word reveals as a powerful part of the arsenal He has given for our triumph in spiritual conflict.

The Song of Breakthrough

The breakthrough of the Gospel into Europe in the first century was supernatural by all criteria.

It began as the result of a Holy Spirit-inspired vision that led Paul and his party to move west instead of east in their evangelistic pursuits.

It was birthed at the edge of a river as God's Word was preached and confirmed by His power as they gained their first European converts.

It was assailed by a repeated and deceptive testimony—shouted from the lips of a demon-possessed woman whose sorceries had gained influence over many in that area.

The sorcerer was delivered from satanic torments when Paul cast the demon from her, setting the woman free to follow Christ.

For their act of mercy, manifest in that act of exorcism, Paul and Silas were cast into prison, a clear effort of the recently expelled demon to restrain further gospel advance into its principality—the doorway to an entire continent.

From within their prison cell, the two beaten-and-bound missionaries began to sing praises to God. Even as they sang, an earthquake shook the area, resulting in the miracle of their jailor's repentance and his whole household's conversion (Acts 16:1-40).

This cluster of events burst like pressed grapes, releasing the wine of Holy Spirit power, and establishing a beachhead for the gospel on a new continent. It seems impossible to cite any single event as pivotal, but one thing shines clearly: the original breakthrough of the gospel westward into Europe was not achieved without an apostolic experience in the sheer power of song.

Not every analyst may relate Paul and Silas' song to their miraculous deliverance from the jail. However, the Bible supports the proposition that such may have been the case and that song is a mighty means of breakthrough and liberation.

> You *are* my hiding place; You shall preserve me from trouble; You shall surround me with songs of deliverance (Psalm 32:7).

> The Lord *is* my strength and song, And He has become my salvation (Exodus 15:2).

> Behold, God *is* my salvation, I will trust and not be afraid; "For YAH, the Lord, *is* my strength and song; He also has become my salvation." Therefore with joy you will draw water From the wells of salvation (Isaiah 12:2–3).

A close examination of these and other passages shows that songs are not only offerings of praise for what God *has* done, but instruments of our present partnering with His almightiness unto deliverance. Psalm 32:7 tells us that the Lord hides us and preserves us from trouble by encircling us with songs of deliverance. Somehow, in ways that defy our analysis, the song of the Lord on the lips of His people has a potential for contributing to spiritual overthrow, upheaval, and breakthrough. Just as music in the physical realm may strike a wavelength that shatters glass, so

songful worship in the spiritual realm can shake Satan's dominion, topple principalities of hell, and extend the Kingdom of
God through Jesus Christ!

Yet one more text reveals another attribute of worship music's
incredible power.

The Song of Birthing

Isaiah 54 opens with a paradoxical command: "Sing, O barren
one!" The irony is that no one would direct a despairing reject to
sing.

In ancient Israel, nothing prompted song less than the barren
condition of a woman. She was disenfranchised, discredited,
suspect of spiritual unworthiness, and potentially subject to
divorce—all on the grounds of her being unable to bear children. Into this depressing situation of personal hopelessness, the
Prophet commands the woman to *sing*; incredibly, with his next
words, he directs her to start preparing a nursery, for there are
babies (plural) coming!

> Enlarge the place of your tent ... For you shall
> expand to the right and to the left, And your descen-
> dants will inherit the nations ... you will forget the
> shame of your youth ... For your Maker *is* your hus-
> band, the Lord of Hosts (Isaiah 54:2–5).

An entire spool of thought unrolls a continuous thread of
blessing that the Lord promises to follow upon the heels of *song
alone!* A tapestry of joy including multiple births is prophesied,
complete with promises of widespread fruit and joyous consequences flowing from the midst of the singer's song. This passage of promise is far more than poetry.

Here is the declaration of a principle that shines from other passages in the Word of God: song and birth—praises and *new life*—are linked together repeatedly. The cause and effect relationship is not always the same, but God being the Author of all that is, the issue raised is not our *sequence in* song but the *suffocation* of song. The Bible reveals that songlessness—depression, defeat, discouragement, despair—restricts the inflow of new life. The spirit of heaviness blankets souls and suffocates hope. However, song has a power to explode despair and expand a space for hope to begin.

From the birth of creation, when God's creative activity was accompanied by music, as "the morning stars sang together, And all the sons of God shouted for joy" (Job 38:7), to the birth-time songs of Hannah and Mary (see 1 Samuel 2:1–10; Luke 1:46–55), songs and new life are joined together. The distinctive thing about Isaiah's words is that the song he calls for is not just a joyous response to a birth; it declares the promise and sets the atmosphere for its fulfillment! It's a possibility in song's sheer dynamic that we may well believe today.

When the Barren Sang

It doubtless seemed "just another Sunday" as Mike and Cheri sat with the congregation that day over a decade ago. I didn't know them at all. They were new to our assembly and it would be a full year until I actually met them.

They probably weren't thinking about the matter that morning, but the fact was, Mike and Cheri were unable to have children. Medical examination had indicated that it was very unlikely they would ever enjoy the parental privilege short of adopting a baby.

Of course, I knew nothing of these facts, nor of their prayerful desire that after eleven years of marriage they might conceive a child.

That day my subject was "The Conceiving and Bearing of Life." It wasn't really a message on having children, but on overcoming any barrenness in the bleak spots of our life. Isaiah 54 was my text, "Sing, O barren," and I discussed God's call to worship and to praise Him at any point of our lives that seems hopelessly unfruitful. It was then that something very special took place.

My understanding of at least one manifestation of the spiritual gift called "a word of knowledge" (1 Corinthians 12:8), is that the Holy Spirit will give someone *both* supernatural insight *and* a corresponding promise from God regarding the issue being revealed. That's exactly what happened while I was preaching. I paused midway in the sermon, sensing the Holy Spirit's presence and prompting, and then I spoke.

"Church," I said, "I need to interrupt myself for just a moment.

"My message has specifically *not* had to do with natural childbearing, but with life flowing into barren parts of our lives in other respects. Still the Holy Spirit is impressing me that there is a couple here this morning who has longed for a child, who has been told they cannot have one, and whom the Lord wants to know He is present to speak to your need in a personal way this morning. His word to you is this: 'Begin to fill your house with song, and as you do, the life-giving power of that song will establish a new atmosphere and make way for the conception that you have desired.'"

I didn't ask anyone to indicate their personal situation or response to that word. Rather, I simply went on with the message as I had planned, basically forgetting about the incident. Until nearly a year later.

I engaged Mike and Cheri in conversation that day at the church, prior to the Sunday they were presenting their baby girl for dedication. Although they had joined our church, I had never had a conversation with them and it was especially nice to talk with them because they were so excited about their baby. After brief opening exchanges, Mike came to the point.

"Pastor Jack, we wanted to talk with you for a few minutes because of this Sunday's dedication of our baby. There's something about it we felt you would want to know … ." With that, he recounted the episode of that Sunday about eleven months before, of their childlessness, their prayer, the Holy Spirit's word to them, and—their baby.

"Pastor," Mike continued, "we went home that day and began to do what the Holy Spirit instructed us—we began to fill our house with song. Cheri and I would walk hand in hand into each room and simply sing praises and worship to the Lord. We just wanted you to know that the baby we're bringing for presentation to the Lord this Sunday is the fruit of that song, that the Lord did fulfill His word given that morning."

Can you imagine how I rejoiced with them?

How gracious our Lord and how tender His ways!

That baby's birth was a holy phenomenon, not conjured up by man's efforts or enthusiasm. It was the precious fruit of one couple's natural union, which, until the divinely appointed song of the Lord entered their situation, had not found the fruitfulness for which they longed.

So, we dedicated the baby. However, there's one last footnote to the story.[4]

It's about Aimee. Remember the little eight-year-old girl who came to the prayer room door and signaled that she wanted to talk with me, and who then sang me the song she said the Lord had given to her?

I was especially touched that morning as little Aimee went back out the door, for as her song was echoing in my ears, I was praising God for the life-begetting power of song. I was reveling in how it can transmit from one generation to another where simple childlike hearts—and congregations—will welcome it.

For, you see, Aimee is Mike and Cheri's daughter. She is the baby who was born because of their "filling the house with song," even though years of barrenness without hope had preceded.

She was the fruit of a song—a song that now was finding a place in her young life.

Who knows what richness her song will bring as her years follow?

Who knows what a new song may bring to you?

12

Beyond All Worlds ...
Here and Now

"Above and beyond all the realm of time and space,
Above earthly limits, beyond this world's embrace,
A life may be found which with power will abound,
If you believe, you can receive power
to live above and beyond."
J.W.H.

To say that he had been born with a silver spoon in his mouth would have exaggerated the point, but there is no doubt that Solomon had an edge on most of his contemporaries. As the beloved Bathsheba's son, he was the living reminder of God's forgiveness and grace toward his father, David. Though he was the second child of a marriage spawned in adultery and murder, the guilt of the past had been flushed away with the tragic death of his brother—the firstborn to this union that was tarnished in its inception and scarred from its establishment.

Now, however, David was dead.

In a flurry of political jockeying, including the diplomatic intervention of Zadok the Priest and Nathan the Prophet, the crown was conferred upon Solomon and the self-seeking takeover attempt of his half-brother Adonijah was averted.

With a humility characteristic of his father, the fledgling ruler sought God's wisdom rather than wealth, and the early stages of his leadership began to be marked with divine blessing.

Solomon finished the Temple.

No greater monument could he build in testimony to the combined devotion of both David and Solomon. The temporary Tabernacle David had established was but a forecast of his highest desire—the hope of building a permanent dwelling place for the manifest presence of the Lord God of Israel. For that which David's planning and financial provision had paved the way, Solomon pursued to completion with equal commitment. On the day of the Temple's dedication, God's pleasure with it all was abundantly clear:

> Then they brought up the ark of the Lord ... [And]
> King Solomon, and all the congregation ... [were]
> sacrificing sheep and oxen that could not be counted
> or numbered for multitude. Then the priests brought
> in the ark of the covenant of the Lord ... And it came
> to pass, when the priests came out of the holy *place,*
> that the cloud filled the house of the Lord, so that
> the priests could not continue ministering because of
> the cloud; for the glory of the Lord filled the house
> of the Lord (1 Kings 8:4–11).

There is no question of God's pleasure with the worship, the worshippers, and the house of worship. The visitation of the Lord and the manifestation of His glory in response to this occasion fully verifies the propriety of it all. Solomon's desire to honor God is confirmed by the Almighty's presence.

The Worthiness of Worship

A special poignancy surrounds that dedication day, especially in the awe-inspired words of Solomon's dedicatory prayer (1 Kings 8:22–54). Kneeling, with his hands spread upward in worship, he brings an impassioned appeal for God's presence, blessing, and mercy to reside among his people. Midway through the prayer, Solomon makes a simple statement that breaks the back of any skeptic's notion that Israel saw Yahweh merely as a tribal deity. Having invited the Lord is abiding presence into the Temple, he says:

> But will God indeed dwell on the earth? Behold,
> heaven and the heaven of heavens cannot contain
> You. How much less this temple which I have built!
> (1 Kings 8:27).

It's here I invite you to pause with me—here at the dedication of Solomon's Temple. To pause meditatively where those words were first spoken, is to be wisely taught, for the worthiness of worship is demonstrated here as in few other places. The event yields a fourfold statement on worth in worship:

1. A *material* declaration of worth is made in the enormous investment the structure represents—all of it being the direct result of offerings brought by devoted worshippers of the Lord.
2. A *spiritual* declaration of worth is seen in the overwhelming number of sacrifices offered that day as they sanctified this new house unto God.
3. A *conceptual* grasp of God's worth is evidenced in Solomon's statement on the grandeur of God's Person

and nature, as his dedicatory prayer acknowledges His omnipotence and transcendence, and rests its faith in the attributes of God's love, mercy, and faithfulness.

4. A *dynamic* demonstration of God's declaration of worth shines forth in His visitation of glory, the seal of His presence, and the affirmation of His acceptance of this worship as truly "worthy."

Keeping Worship "Worthy"

There is a two-edged problem in seeking to ensure our worship is sufficiently worthy.

On the one hand, there is a contemporary tendency toward the inappropriately casual, which may claim to be simple but actually becomes trite, glib, and occasionally "cutesy" at times of praise and worship. Even the most sincere leader can contribute to the evolution of a less-than-worthy view of God among those he leads unless cautioned against the possibility of people misreading his casual style. The desire to sustain a bright, positive atmosphere can too easily destroy occasions for deep, heart-searching, and holy contemplation of God's greatness and holiness. An upbeat spirit and mood is appropriate—assuming it doesn't beget a deadbeat slovenliness of mind toward God's Person and glorious attributes. However, since a predisposition toward the informal can unwittingly cultivate an insensitivity toward the One to Whom worshippers come, I want to lead toward, and to participate in, worship that commands our entire thought, our most sensitive devotion, and our reverential fear.

On the other hand, some react strongly to perceived shallowness allowed in certain settings. I must be careful to guard against criticizing those without the theological enlightenment I may feel important to worthy worship. Such a reaction can produce a self-righteous quest for excellence, which may easily dissolve into an equal, though opposite, carnality.

Pride is not superior to shallowness and perceived super-ficiality cannot effectively be countered by labored efforts at being "deep." Depth is not the product of brainpower or social style, but only results from a genuine desire for God's honor and not a vindication of viewpoint. However great my devotion to "re-dignifying" worship, God will *never* be impressed by my "worthy" efforts if they smack of a secret sense of superiority above the worship style of any other of His children.

Weorthscipe

Weorthscipe. That Old English word meant "to ascribe worth, to pay homage, to reverence, or to venerate." It inevitably turns up in any search for the real meaning of worship, for it addresses the issue of worth—of ascribed *worthiness* in worship—and it asks questions of us who worship.

1. What value are you placing here? Is the manner of hon-oring the One you are worshipping proportionate to His character and attributes?
2. Do the praises of worshippers indicate their awareness of the traits inherent in the One they extol? What is pres-ent of adoration—of plain, heartfelt, emotional love and affection?
3. Does the worship involve genuine devotion, or is it only an intellectual exercise—in *truth* but not in Spirit? The fuel of our worship may be our understanding, but the fires of worship are ignited from the heart, and not the mind.

How shall we bring worthy worship to the Most Worthy One?

Solomon's Temple is a good place to come to learn of *weorthscipe*. It is the scene where three great themes of worship took place, all of which emphasize God's worthiness and necessitate a "reformation." Consider the *transcendence*, the *transaction*, and the *transformation* involved in worthy worship.

The Transcendence of God

God's transcendence describes His *beyondness*. Though He is present everywhere, He is also beyond all worlds. He who created all things is separate from and existent beyond His creation. When we say God is present *in* the midst of His creation it is not the same as saying He is present *within* it. The *first* makes Him our present help—the truly personal being He is—who desires to dwell among His own, and to manifest His love and power in their interest. *The second* depersonalizes Him, claiming to contain Him within His own handiwork, as though God was literally in the fragrance of flowers, the tenderness of a baby, or the grandeur of the starry heavens.

It is an error that anyone supposes God to be a *part* of His own creation, but it is also an error to suppose it an exaltation of His greatness to forget or neglect the truth of His immediacy—because He is personally interested in, cares for, and is with each of us.

We should take time in our worship to know and enjoy the wonder of God's personal attributes. Entire books are written on each aspect of His nature, each quality of His character, and each attribute of His being—for there is no way the marvel of God's greatness can be exhausted by human analysis. Still, theological expertise isn't a prerequisite to worship God, but a hunger to know Him is. Intellectualizing God's traits does not certify a worthier worship, but passive indifference or mere excitement will miss the mark, too. God calls us to neither a mind-trip nor an emotional binge. Let Holy Spirit-filled worship be a blend of our highest thoughts and our deepest feelings, so that we can reach the goal of true worship: *the reshaping of our lives.*

Because human nature inevitably becomes like the object of its worship, an ever-deepening perspective on our Father's nature enhances the likelihood of those qualities forming in us. Thoughtful comment by sensitive worship leaders can stimulate such growth, expanding the praise and increasing the insight of those who join them in worship. Well-stated, concise remarks in introducing a chorus or hymn help in this regard.

Anna is unusually gifted at this.

It is common, on a Sunday morning, as my wife leads our people in the selected hymn of the day, for her to pause between two verses and make a personal observation or relate a pithy anecdote. The effect is often dramatic and the next verse ignites as an aspect of God's goodness is refreshed in our thoughts. The secret to her effectiveness is her simplicity and brevity. She knows this is no time for a homily, but her sensitivity overflows and awakens sensitivity in the whole congregation.

Let us learn to meditate on God's power, His love, His wisdom, His holiness, His changelessness, His mercy, His glory. You might have the opportunity to invite other worshippers to do so with you. "Let's pause before we sing this again, and let the Holy Spirit help you recall some way in which God's *almightiness* has met you at specific points." (You could do the same with any trait appropriate to a hymn, chorus, or other song.) His personal traits will be most quickly perceived when related to the worshipper's experience rather than related only as theological concepts. Living worship can be set aflame when sparked by expanding perspectives on our Father's attributes. An increased deepening of praise, worship, and thanksgiving is inevitable where worshippers are led to think on the manifold splendor of the Eternal One—our God. Let us kneel to worship ... Let us rise to praise ...

> The Almighty and Self-Sufficient One,
> The Entirely Holy Three-In-One,
> The Merciful, The Righteous, and The Just,
> The All-Knowing and All-Wise,
> The Essence and Fountain of Love,
> The Creator and Lord of Hosts,
> The Absolute and Changeless One,
> The Transcendent and The Immanent One,
> The True and Faithful One,

Who, in all His wonder, grandeur, and excellence,
> has chosen to love us, and
> has sought to redeem us, and
> has sent His Son to us.

JESUS CHRIST
THE ONE AND ONLY SAVIOR

He has become our Father through the new birth
> He has made possible in Christ,
>> who was born of the virgin,
>> who lived sinlessly,
>> taught truthfully, and
>> died vicariously for mankind.
> Whose blood and death are the ransom price paid for me—
>> providing completely for my eternal salvation.
He is the Son of God,

Who literally and physically rose from the dead,
Who has ascended to the right hand of the Majesty
   on High, and
Who has poured out His Holy Spirit of power upon us,
   That we might live in grace both now and forever
Let the Father be praised!
Let His Son be worshipped!
Let His Spirit be manifest among us!

Our Transactions with God

Worthy worship begins with its focus on the greatness of God and His goodness to us. However, there is a critical juncture at which worship requires a transaction—that a very real piece of business take place.

Sacrifice. Offering. There is no such thing as worship without there being something very tangible brought from man's side.

Worship may be fulfilling, enriching, soul-stirring, enlightening, healing, refreshing, restful, invigorating—or any one of the innumerable other beneficial results that heartfelt worship realizes. However, because God doesn't require payment for His blessings and because His gifts cannot be bought, worship can become a joy to our souls, a healing to our hearts, and a balm to our minds, and yet we still have not made any definitive investment ourselves. As filled with blessing and beauty as such worship may be for a season, if worshippers do not come to understand their responsibility in giving, the loveliest worship will eventually evaporate into thin air and thin souls.

Solomon's Temple reminds us that worthy worship involves a material investment. It is significant that this glorious structure, so overflowing with God's far more glorious presence, was built on the site of a business transaction made by his father

David—a transaction made in the interest of worship. The Temple was constructed on land that had already become a place of a redemptive sacrifice in worship and of a willing sacrifice of wealth. David said to Araunah as he sought to secure the property for the purpose of sacrifice to God, "I will not offer to the Lord my God that which costs me nothing" (2 Samuel 24:24 author's paraphrase). Araunah's offer to freely give his King the land was graciously rejected by David. He knew worship should have a worthiness including an open hand as well as an open heart.

There is no escaping our need to affirm repeatedly the principle of tangible, material giving being properly associated with worship under the New Covenant. Human nature instinctively fears giving. It is not so much stinginess as self-protection, and our worship of God is a means for our deliverance from that fear—if we'll accept it. The cost is our honest confrontation of any residual fear of giving. The tender teaching of the truth, spoken in the spirit of God's love for us all, can set people free to give in worship and to live in worshipful generosity.

The offering of an animal under the Old Testament order was symbolic of Christ's sacrifice for our sin. The grace it promises was not being bought thereby, but being anticipated. Because of this, we often overlook a very basic fact. Essentially, the ancient sacrifices were a "cash" transaction. In an agricultural society, nothing was a more specific expenditure of personal property than presenting an animal from your herd. As obvious as this is, hosts of New Testament believers live out a relatively unsacrificial lifestyle in terms of their worship transactions.

At times there seems to be undue diligence in the attempt to demolish biblical disciplines about money. No subject was more debated or subjected to personal interpretation than church giving—offerings, tithes, special funds, etc. A basic tendency is as persistent today as it was in Cain and Abel's day. While some give obediently, others still insist on their own opinions and demand that God receive their offerings on their own terms. Appealing to our no longer being "under the law" regarding financial sacrifice seems to violate the concept of "grace." Peculiarly, some contend on the grounds of the New Testament for the abolition of the discipline of the tithe. They assail tithing as though its teaching were a dangerous legalism rather than a liberating truth. I've seen worshippers, who are enjoying a reformation in freeing song and praise, suddenly wince when tithes and offerings are collected—as though it were a materialistic degradation of their "pure worship," an imposition of legalistic demands on otherwise liberated believers. That's not a reformation: it's a rebellion!

Truly reformed, biblical worship is not secure in our souls until it cuts across our fear and our selfishness. Planned, persistent, disciplined, faithful, obedient giving is the sword that can cut away superficiality, loose us from doubt and disobedience, and cause the spirit of sacrifice to fuel a revival in our lives.

Tithes and offerings are as incumbent upon the New Testament believer as upon worshippers in earlier eras. Why?

1. Jesus Himself confirmed the practice of tithing as being valid, joining to it the high promise of God's abundance being poured back upon His disciples, who would learn the release that comes through worshipful giving (Matthew 23:23; Luke 6:38).
2. New Testament believers are called to walk in the steps of Abraham, the first Bible character to practice tithing as a response to God's blessing upon his life (Romans 4:12; Hebrews 7:4–6; Genesis 14:18–22).

3. Systematic and proportional giving were taught in the Gentile church as disciplines releasing the ministry of the Church to serve human need. This was done willingly even though almost all Old Testament ordinances were not required of them (1 Corinthians 16:2; Acts 15:22–29).

4. The glory of the New Covenant at no point retreats from the character values of the Old, but enhances and expands them. In terms of giving, we would logically expect an increase, or at the very least, no retreat or reduction of disciplined giving patterns (2 Corinthians 3:9,11).

5. There are blessings promised related to the giving of tithes and offerings. They are not less applicable because they are in the Old Testament (2 Corinthians 1:20; Malachi 3:8–12).

The transaction of tithes and offerings is no small issue. Where people are experiencing reform in worship, giving increases dramatically. If it doesn't, the worship reformation may not be suspect, but it will be short-lived. Tithing and giving may not guarantee the presence of a spirit of worship, but their absence can guarantee its eventual withering.

However, there's even more to this matter of worship's transaction. Today's reform is fostering a return in the Church to biblical freedom in the physical expressions of worship everywhere. A fresh look at Romans 12:1 is alerting us to the New Testament sacrifice of our *bodies*—another confrontation with our fears.

I beseech you therefore, brethren, by the mercies of God, that you present your bodies a living sacrifice, holy, acceptable to God, which is your reasonable service (Romans 12:1).

Just the other day I had the privilege of watching one of the executives in our congregation present a seminar for other executives. This man represents one of today's best-known corporations and travels internationally to help them solve their problems. As he began the seminar with these cool-headed, calculating executives, he said, "I'm going to ask for your response. I'm going to want you to show me some skin." What he meant was that he wanted them to signal with their hands when they responded. He wanted them to actuate and activate their responses. When we come to worship the Lord, I think He would say the same thing to us, "Show Me some skin." The Lord wants us to demonstrate our response to Him, and He wants us to use our bodies to do so.

The Bible is very explicit that our bodies are to be involved in worship. In Psalm 50:5 the Lord says, "Gather My saints together to Me, Those who have made a covenant with Me by sacrifice." In the Old Testament, worshippers offered sacrifices of animals and grain, but that was not all that was required. The worshipper also came with praise and thanksgiving. Psalm 107:22 tells us explicitly that thanksgiving is a sacrifice to the Lord.

In Philippians 2:17, Paul speaks of himself as being a sacrifice. Of course, when Paul wrote to the Philippians, he was in prison and he knew he could be facing death. This is perhaps the most dramatic example of sacrifice. There are people in the world who face having to make that literal sacrifice of their lives, but all of us can apply that verse to our lives along with Romans 12:1.

God expects nothing less than complete sacrifice of ourselves to Him. What has traditionally been absent or categorically written off as "calisthenics" practiced by certain "sects," is now being accepted as timeless and valid for us all. Many of us are learning to include another transaction in our worship—the offering of our bodies in a sacrifice of *physical* expressions of praise humbly presented in worship.

Kneeling is becoming more widely practiced during the worship and singing of evangelical Protestants. We often avoided this practice due to perceiving it as too "high church" or "Catholic," and reserved only for a penitent at the altar following an invitation. Now its practice is filling our worship, and not only in our prayer meetings. Such songs as "Come Let Us Worship and Bow Down" point the way and encourage us to do what we are singing.

Upraised hands, once resisted by most of the Church and consigned to oblivion by all but Pentecostals and Charismatics, is realizing a beautiful and orderly use everywhere. People are responding to the apostle Paul's wish: "I desire therefore that the men pray everywhere, lifting up holy hands" (1 Timothy 2:8).

Applause and rhythmic handclapping, the most natural physical expression of human joyfulness, are acceptable in an increasing circle of the faithful. Once deemed irreverent or superficial, the reformation is not only applying the biblical commandment to offer such praises, but also allowing the possibility that such humanness as "clapping for joy" is a God-created tendency put within man, and therefore appropriate for praising Him.

These physical expressions are part of the transaction of worship because they actually involve an investment—the spending of more of our whole selves, presenting our bodies, often at the expense of our pride. A holy liberation is unleashing a full-spectrum worship, expressed by the awakening of the *whole human being*—spirit, soul, mind, *and* body.

Our Transformation Before God

God gave the glorious manifestation of His presence at the dedication of Solomon's Temple as more than merely a resplendent, awe-inspiring sight. The Scriptures reveal God's glory as meant *for* us—to touch us, to affect us, and to transform us.

The ultimate purpose in God's glory shown toward man is shown in Jesus Christ. He is God's conclusive display of glory, and with His coming, we see the qualities and purpose of that glory:

> And the Word became flesh and dwelt [literally tabernacled] among us, and we beheld His glory, the glory as of the only begotten of the Father, full of grace and truth (John 1:14).

His glory—filled with grace and truth—makes God's glory not only our object in worship, but also our source of blessing. He gives His glory to overflow us with grace and truth. Grace meets us where we are and truth sets us free to become! He gives His glory to transform us, not to entertain us. Where bruise, bondage, or affliction are present, worship welcomes the glory of God—His excellence of power to redeem, restore, and reinstate.

> Where the Spirit of the Lord *is* there *is* liberty. But we all, with unveiled face, beholding as in a mirror the glory of the Lord, are being transformed into the same image from glory to glory, just as by the Spirit of the Lord (2 Corinthians 3:17–18).

He who transcends all worlds comes to transform us. He is here to liberate—to scatter our fears, overthrow our doubt, strengthen our weakness, and explode sin and self-imposed restrictions.

Our worship is His means to lift us out of ourselves, *not* to some euphoric mysticism, cultish meditation, demonic astral travel, or humanistic quest for supra-consciousness.

Instead, He invites us to come before His throne and permit the glory of His power to change our hearts, our attitudes, our thought patterns, our character deficiencies. He wants to transform us, turning:

- our fears into our resting in His love
- our pride into our waiting at His feet
- our weakness into our discovery of His grace
- our pain into a healing of our whole personality
- our doubt into a new faith in His faithfulness.

That's what worship's transformation is. It is God's way to transmit wholeness, and our coming to realize the meaning of worshipping, "in the beauty of holiness."

Holy, Holy, Holy

It was a century and a half after Solomon stood within the courts of the newly finished Temple that another young man was at worship in the same building. Suddenly, captivated by the spirit of worship, Isaiah saw a vision of the Lord.

> I saw the Lord sitting on a throne, high and lifted up, and the train of His *robe* filled the temple (Isaiah 6:1).

He continues by describing the angelic beings worshipping around the Creator's throne, who ceaselessly lift their voices in continuous praise.

Holy, holy, holy *is* the Lord of hosts;
The whole earth *is* full of His glory! (Isaiah 6:3).

Isaiah relates his suddenly being stricken with a sense of his unworthiness as the pure power of God's presence shakes the place.

Woe *is* me, for I am undone!
Because I *am* a man of unclean lips
And I dwell in the midst of a people of unclean lips;
For my eyes have seen the King,
The Lord of hosts (Isaiah 6:5).

As Isaiah looks upon the holiness of the Almighty, His awe in worship suddenly turns to shame for sin. He becomes deeply aware of all of the things he *isn't,* as he looks upon all the things God is. What follows is as heart-touching a scene as any in the Bible, for it provides a lovely study in the transforming power of worship. The response of the Most Holy God to that worshipper's confession is as mighty in meaning as it is merciful in manner.

Isaiah had confessed the impurity of his lips, and the words of despair have hardly been spoken when instantly—without a word of condemnation or a moment of hesitation—the Living God responds. God commissions an angel to take a coal from heaven's altar and apply its purifying flame to the point of Isaiah's confessed need and concern.

Truth flashes here like lightning!

The prophet's experience teaches us for all time that our failures are not barricades to our approaching the Holy One. Worship allows the unworthy to come before God in the full expectation that His holy wholeness will answer to our un-whole un-holiness. Just as with Isaiah, living worship will increase our sense of His holiness and our unworthiness, and make room for a transforming encounter that will purge our sin. Isaiah found the fire of God applied to the specific point of his need, and we can expect the same. God will halt the flow of sin from any part of our life.

With Isaiah, it was his lips.

Where do you need purifying? At the cross we find saving forgiveness through Christ's Blood, but at the altar of worship we can find sanctifying holiness through the Holy Spirit's fire. Encounters like Isaiah's receive the assurance of God's love, forgiveness for sin, and direction for the future. In such transforming worship, God reveals the way His transcendent, glorious holiness has come to penetrate our world.

Hear it! See It! Isaiah invites us all to share his encounter with God's glory.

Listen—loved one!

Glory is what we all lost when we lost touch with God.

Glory is what we all seek—the recovery of that loss.

However, our fumbling, bumbling ways of going about regaining it are a study in human frustration and human sin. Man seeks glory down labyrinthine ways of selfish, willful, prideful, and blind pursuits. The quest for what we might become is so often outside the presence of the very One who holds the key to our becoming.

Now He invites us to glory.

The heavenly call to worship is not the demanding directive of a deity concerned for His own glory. His call to come into His glorious presence is born of His concern over *our* glory, and His desire to restore our glory by our welcoming His. God is ready to pour His glory upon us, purge us with its fire, overflow us with its power, and bring us to His created purpose for our lives!

That's why He keeps saying, "Remember."

13

Remembering What
to Remember

"Until He comes again, His death will I proclaim.
I will eat this bread and I will drink this wine,
Until He comes again ... Until He comes again."
J.W.H.

WE WERE LATE for church.

As we rather apologetically slipped into the row, our five-year-old son, Mark, slid onto the seat next to mine. Anna and I were both somewhat bleary-eyed. The whole family had just suffered a post-Christmas siege of flu, and we had thought at first we would stay home that morning. Either guilt or grace, I don't know which, got us going in time to at least make the last service.

It was New Year's Sunday. I didn't know a miracle was about to happen.

Communion is always served at our church on the first Sunday of the month. We call it communion or the Lord's Table. For others it's called the Eucharist or the Mass, and it is observed at widely differing intervals and in very different ways, depending upon which group you worship with. As it turned out, this time for us was to become very memorable.

At that time, I was teaching at LIFE Bible College and had no pastoral duties on Sunday. Our tardy family sat near the back row in Angelus Temple's spacious auditorium when communion began. As the pastor read the Scripture, I listened again to the apostle Paul's instruction:

> For I received from the Lord that which I also delivered to you: that the Lord Jesus on the *same* night in which He was betrayed took bread; and when He had given thanks, He broke *it* and said, "Take, eat; this is My body which is broken for you; do this in *remembrance of Me*. In the same manner *He* also *took* the cup after supper, saying, "This cup is the new covenant in My blood. This do, as often as you drink *it*, in *remembrance of Me*. For as often as you eat this bread and drink this cup, you proclaim the Lord's death till He comes (1 Corinthians 11:23–26 emphasis added).

The passage refreshed my memory of the fact Paul had called this event a proclamation, a declaration—literally; a *preaching* of Christ ... until He returns again.[1] The Greek verb *is* dramatic in its etymology—*katangello*—the second part of the verb being the same word as "angel." Somehow, that dramatizes the *message-bearing* potential implicit in the action. Paul taught that it is a proclamation, a sermon, a message, a preachment. It's a message of *life* centered in a commemoration of a death. The morning worship continued.

Prayer was offered, and as the congregation praised God for the provisions of the Cross, a spirit of expectancy filled the room. While ushers began distributing the bread and the cup, we sang a chorus of exaltation to Jesus Himself.

There were more people there than on an average Lord's Day—there always was on communion Sunday. Our people seemed to appreciate the *life* and *joy* this feature of worship always held when we celebrated The Table.

My mind turned to my son seated beside me, at age five appearing rather oblivious to the proceedings of the made-for-adults service in progress. We were so late we'd opted against dropping him off in children's church. We were shortly to discover the gracious providence in that decision.

"Son," I said, anticipating the arrival of the bread tray being passed down the row just ahead of us, "do you know what we're all doing right now?" He looked at me rather blankly; his expression indicated that he really didn't notice *anything* that was happening.

I continued, "We're having communion today, and Daddy's going to help you so you can take communion with the rest of the people."

He brightened, looking expectant. "Good." I smiled, wondering how much of Mark's response might be his knowing he was going to get to drink from "one of those little glasses." Then, somehow, I began to sense this was to be an unusual moment. I wondered if I shouldn't take time—then and there—to help him understand about "those little bits of crackers and tiny cups."

I took two pieces of the bread in my hand, and as the tray came with the cups, I nodded to the usher.

"I'm explaining communion to my son," I whispered. "I'll return the cups after the service."

The elderly man recognized me, smiled graciously, and moved on without interrupting what turned out to be a miracle moment in our family's life.

Communion is always special, and New Year's Sunday always has a "brand-newness" written all over it. However, before this New Year's communion day was over, I would be walking home beside my son—both of us having shared a distinctly joyous experience.

Mark received Jesus Christ as his Savior that morning!

To this day if you ask Mark—who is a husband, a father of twins, and a pastor himself—he'll tell you he received Christ when he was five years old. Worshipping with his dad. At a communion service. On New Year's Sunday morning a long time ago.

Of course, Mark wouldn't say—now *or* then—that he was born again *through* taking communion. Anyone understanding God's Word knows that participating in a Christian ordinance doesn't *gain* salvation. However, the Lord's Table does *preach* it, and Mark heard the message loud and clear that day. It happened as people worshipped in an atmosphere of faith, fullness, and joy and as I took time to explain the message in the elements.

"Mark, this bread is to remind us of Jesus' body. This cup of grape juice is to remind us of Jesus' blood." I spoke slowly, watching his response as I sought to help him understand the importance of partaking.

"We *want* the Lord Jesus to live inside us *all* the time, son." He recognized the distinction between a moment's observance of a ritual and the continuing indwelling of a reality.

I was being careful, not wanting either to press beyond his ability to understand or to push beyond the Holy Spirit's dimension of dealing with the young boy's heart. Nevertheless, it was God's moment for Mark, and as He arranged it that way, everything merged into a precious, memorable experience for a dad. My little boy really was saved that day! He really *did* understand, and he really *did* receive Christ!

Jesus' Skin?

The service had concluded now, and as I walked to the front of the sanctuary to return the two cups, I invited Mark to walk with me.

In our tradition, it is common for those who respond to an evangelistic invitation to come forward for prayer and counseling. As we finished taking the bread and the cup, I had said to Mark, "Now that you've received the Lord Jesus into your heart, would you like to go up to the front and tell Dr. Duffield?" He had smiled and brightly acknowledged his desire to do so, and now we were there.

It was tenderly significant that this same man, who five years before had held Mark in his arms and presented him to the Lord in dedication as Anna and I brought our baby before the congregation, was about to hear of another birth. He had just finished exchanging remarks with one of the congregation, and then turned to us.

"Good morning, Jack." Then, grinning, "How are you, Mark? Did you have a nice Christmas?"

Mark responded with a child's usual bashfulness, and I lifted him up on the altar rail so he could speak face to face with the pastor.

I handed Dr. Duffield the two communion cups, explaining, "We just had a very special time at communion, and Mark wanted to tell you what happened."

"Son," I said, turning to him, "tell Dr. Duffield what you did a few minutes ago."

The small boy straightened, and with crystal clarity in his eyes, looked into the face of the older man. Then, with a singular certainty that only the Holy Spirit can bring to *any* heart—a child's as well—he said, "I asked Jesus to come into my heart."

Dr. Duffield was genuine in his joy. "Mark, that's wonderful. I'm so glad for that." His responsiveness clearly showed my son that his decision was as credible as any adult's was. "I'm so happy you came to tell me." Then with gentle pastoral sensitivity, he took the boy's hand and offered a prayer of thanksgiving and assurance.

When we had finished, I thought I'd quiz Mark to let him show how well he knew what the elements of the communion table represented. Taking a piece of broken bread from one of the trays at the table nearby, I gave it to him and asked, "Can you tell Dr. Duffield what this stands for?" His answer has become a classic family story and it disrupted any possibility of sanctimony residing in the moment.

"This is Jesus' *skin!*"

Dr. Duffield and I exploded in laughter, our amusement over Mark's choice of terms being something of a bewilderment to the boy. I explained the difference between "body" and skin to Mark, and then we said good-bye. Taking my son's hand, I started up the aisle thinking how grateful I was—so thankful to be a part of a church that worshipped with power and also kept communion's meaning before its people.

A Lost Focus

"In Remembrance of Me" is carved into the front of a million tables in a million sanctuaries around the world; the Lord's Table is the most thoroughly established tradition on this planet. In terms of the frequency of its observance and the sheer number who participate in it, communion doesn't have a vital counterpart anywhere. If there is any single, central point of Christian worship, it's the Lord's Table. It is also a central point of needed reform, because of a common problem of lost focus in its observance.

When Jesus said, "This do in remembrance of Me," He obviously was addressing the human inclination to forget, but it is not as obvious, nor is it as well defined, what He wanted us to remember. I'm convinced that much of the Church has a reverse view on the central point of Jesus' command, and the difference is between *life* and *death*.

Of course, any lost focus isn't due to a lack of intelligence. There are greater minds than mine presiding over The Table at many locations in the Church. However, I do feel that a preoccupation with the details of the *history* of Jesus' passion supplants His intent—that we remember the *victory* He won. I think a new reformation needs to influence the mood of our celebration, and that can only precipitate from a fresh assessment of Christ's *meaning* in instituting The Table. I'll answer these questions later, but let me stir thought with them as a starting place:

1. What is it Christ wants us to remember at His Table?
2. How best can we practice "thanksgiving" (the meaning of *eucharist*)?
3. What mood ought to characterize the receiving of communion?
4. How can *worship* at The Table become a *witness* of His power?

A good beginning for any reform at the Lord's Table might be in our studying the first reform ever applied to it. It wasn't in Europe in the sixteenth century but in Corinth in the first. The issue then was also one of lost focus, and a look at Paul's dealing with the Corinthians provides very workable insights for worshipping at the Lord's Table.

> Now in giving these instructions I do not praise *you*, since you come together not for the better but for the worse. For first of all, when you come together as a church, I hear that there are divisions among you, and in part I believe it. For there must also be

factions among you, that those who are approved
may be recognized among you. Therefore, when you
come together in one place, it is not to eat the Lord's
Supper. For in eating, each one takes his own supper
ahead of *others*; and one is hungry and another is
drunk. What! Do you not have houses to eat and
drink in? Or do you despise the church of God and
shame those who have nothing? What shall I say to
you? Shall I praise you in this? I do not praise *you*
(1 Corinthians 11:17–22).

The people in Corinth had become confused about a number
of matters concerning the believer's lifestyle and worship. Since
the Lord's Table is so central to New Testament worship, it's
not surprising that they needed correction there too. The apostle's approach to their many problems was consistently direct
and patient. In writing to correct and adjust, he acknowledges
their unusual vulnerability to confusion due to their past: "You
know that you were Gentiles, carried away to these dumb idols,
however you were led" (one Corinthians 12:2). Their background had colored and altered several foundational aspects of
their life as believers and the Lord's Table was just one example.
Communion-time had become party-time.

One might first question how so meaningful an observance as
the Lord's Table could ever have become so warped. Their now
confused practice, which Paul claims to have originally introduced to them in a pure form, had become a cross between a
picnic and a social spree. The context shows that some worshippers were being completely left out, while others were feasting as
though the event were a bizarre banquet rather than a memorial
to Jesus Christ. They had obviously forgotten at least one thing
they were supposed to remember—Christ's Body is *one*. Not

only had irreverence taken over, but there was disunity and self-ishness at The Table. Incredible!

It was as though invitations read, "B.Y.O.D.—Bring Your Own Dinner! If you don't have it with you, you won't get any from me!"[2] Paul had to cool what had become wild enthusiasm, and correct what had become rampant self-centeredness.

Apostolic correction was necessary, of course. However, it seems that even to this day a residue of reticence lingers around anything Paul corrected in Corinth. If they exaggerated it, the assignment in our time, it seems, is to underplay it. The degree to which we fear being "Corinthian" is not so much reflected in our balance as in our equally exaggerated and opposite extreme. It has become more traditional to scorn fornicators than to scold and then to restore them. It is more acceptable to skip "tongues" altogether than to venture the possibility. Corinthian ignorance on a theme seems to breed contemporary ignoring of the same, and this seems to be the case in the Church's general approach to the Lord's Table.

It appears that our reaction to the Corinthians' confusion has bred an historic Church-wide reluctance at *celebration*—to really be *happy* at communion.

The remedial action Paul took against foolish extremes seems to have been interpreted as an outright insistence that communion be always observed with cool reserve. It's rare to discover actual *rejoicing* at the Lord's Table. Forthright praise or a plain show of human joyfulness tends to be interpreted as potentially irreverent—risky of a Corinthian recurrence. Today, far too often, what Jesus left as the Church's *Thanksgiving Dinner* has become more of a post-funeral one. Rather than celebrating a harvest, something of a pall hangs over The Table.

However, communion is a harvest time celebration!

Jesus was sown as a seed-unto-death and has been raised again as the firstfruits of resurrection-life-triumph! Yet, instead of our celebrating a harvest of life, our observances often seem more like a gathering of loved ones at a post-interment dinner where it is customary for family members to speak in hushed tones of the one just buried. Peculiarly enough, communion is often "celebrated" in this same heaviness of spirit—a practice that has virtually been sanctified as though it were the essence of reverence.

I propose that the Corinthians' loss of focus is not without a contemporary parallel. However, where theirs was a loss of perspective on reverence, I think ours has become a misinterpretation of reverence. Joy, triumph, and a visitation of divine power hardly seem allowable, and yet the celebration of Christ's Cross ought to occasion the "preaching" of all three—with a presiding spirit of victory.

Some questions may help us understand to what degree we may need a reformation in worship at the Lord's Table. Do I find the music employed at communion to be always subdued if not dirge-like? Is it common that an unnatural somberness prevails? Has something of an exaggerated concern for a machinelike distribution of the elements become more important than a sense of a corporate partaking *together*—somehow reducing to private activity what is ideally an occasion of being *gathered for power*? Have you ever sensed the occasion seeming more to breed guilt than to release deliverances? Have you witnessed The Table ever becoming a battleground of separation rather than holy ground where there is an invitation to life, forgiveness, and unity?

Verbal or Vital?

What is it that Christ wants us to remember at His Table?

We know the *verbal* answer—*Him*: "This do in remembrance of *Me*." However, the verbal answer is not the same as the *vital* answer, and in no way automatically insures our grasping the *real* point in communion. If we can receive it, I believe Paul's words focus for us precisely what Jesus had in mind: "As often as you eat this bread and drink this cup *you proclaim the Lord's death* until He comes."

What is he proposing in this proclamation of Jesus' dying? Is this a call to retell the *story* of the Crucifixion—to reenact the *suffering* He underwent—or is it to declare the *fruit* of His death? Based on the mere words it could appear that "Don't forget Jesus' death" meant a solemn, ritual review of Calvary. However, I think reason recommends that Christ meant us to observe more than a morbid, funereal, commemorative service.

I don't think anything like that *ever* existed in *any* first-century congregation.

If a commemoration of death was what Jesus had in mind, and if that's what the Early Church celebrated, then there is no rational explanation as to how the Corinthians ever arrived at so exaggerated a feast. However, if earlier believers celebrated Christ's death with joy, remembering the Cross as the God-given key to *life*, then it becomes plausible how a carnal, pagan-just-turned-Christian community might have distorted so joyous a feast. If Paul had instituted a somber, contemplative observance of The Table, it seems unlikely that the festivities could have so evolved. However, if under Paul's founding leadership the Corinthians had been led to the Lord's Table as an occasion for remembering (1) the triumph of the cross, (2) the power of its provision, and (3) the joy of our hope, and if the celebration were focused on what Jesus *finished* for us at Calvary, then a disposition toward *feasting* makes sense. We can then imagine, with the passage of the five years between Paul's pastorate in Corinth and his first epistle to them, that a young church newly birthed out of a Bacchanalian culture might lose its balance.

I propose that the Early Church celebrated The Table as a positive, pointed, reverently rejoicing, power-filled celebration of Christ's Cross. Even though it might have deteriorated into a self-centered feast in Corinth, I doubt Paul—or God—ever intended the pendulum to swing to the other extreme. I think a reformation in worship needs to come to the Lord's Table and shake off the shackles of suffocating morbidity. I think we need to define more specifically the reason for the Lord Jesus' concern that we "remember" Him. This is more crucial than some may suppose, because a funereal approach to Christ's Table is not only depressing, it almost suggests a neurotic's self-centeredness in Jesus' words, "Remember Me"—an appeal that would be unworthy of *anyone*, much less the Son of God.

To observe the mood of some communion services I've conducted in my past, one would think the object was to pacify a God who was still irritated that we caused Him so much inconvenience and injury. In commanding, "Remember Me," did Jesus mean to direct us to periodically commiserate together and remember how badly the Cross hurt Him? Did He mean to call us to His Table to ceaselessly hound us? "Remember, it's your fault I had to go through all this, and I don't want you to ever forget it!" Have you ever witnessed communion observances that seemed more geared to self-flagellation than holy celebration? What can we do?

What Can We Do?

To begin, let's help worshippers distinguish the difference between somberness and sobriety. The two are often blurred, somewhat like reverence has been made synonymous with silence. The *somberness* often dominating communion is depressing, while a healthy sobriety of heart can be discerning. The latter is appropriate, but one questions if the former *ever* is.

Of course, some occasions will be more subdued than others. For example, Good Friday services usually include the entire recounting of Jesus' death and suffering. Such sensitive commemoration is certainly appropriate and desirable. I personally observe a three-day fast every year leading up to Good Friday; essentially a means of helping me remember Jesus' passion for me. I *do believe* a sensible soul will periodically reflect on the physical agony and emotional anguish Jesus experienced for us in giving His life. However, in the main, it seems difficult to suppose Jesus ever meant our regular communion "remembrance" to focus on His agony, in a way that would instill guilt in our souls and an atmosphere of defeat. We surely must *never* take His suffering lightly, for the Cross was a grotesque, torturous event, but "remembering Him" doesn't require reliving its horror.

I submit that the Bible evidences that Jesus' "Remember Me" calls for a victorious, regular remembrance, focused on the accomplishments of His Cross. I propose that Paul, in directing us to "proclaim the Lord's death until He comes," meant the *proclamation* to be the same *good news* Jesus announced in His own ministry. Calvary has obtained and accentuated this message of hope and promise: "The Spirit of the Lord *is* upon Me, Because He has anointed Me to preach the gospel to *the* poor … to heal the brokenhearted, To proclaim liberty to *the* captives, And recovery of sight to *the* blind, To set at liberty those who are oppressed" (Luke 4:18)."

Isn't it more likely that if Jesus were to preside next Sunday at His Table where we worship, He would say: "While you're partaking, *I want you to remember what I've secured for you.*" He would want you to:

- enjoy every benefit of forgiveness
- receive every provision of victory
- enter into freedom from every point of bondage
- partake of His healing presence and power

Of course He doesn't want us to forget!

Of course He would say, "Remember!" He suffered death to make it all possible and His Table is His way of keeping the provisions of Calvary constantly before us. Our Great Shepherd has prepared a table before us in the presence of our enemies, and He invites us to it in order to anoint our heads with oil so that our cup of rejoicing may overflow (Psalm 23:5).

We are *not* serving a neurotic Savior summoning our nostalgia. To urge the spirit of celebration at His Table is not to suggest we are becoming casual about Calvary. On the contrary, we come to His Table with joy to exalt His Name for His massive victory there. We must replace a medieval mindset of morbidity and false reverence at the Lord's Table with one of holy celebration. To point the way, I propose these answers to the questions I presented earlier in this chapter. Maybe they can constitute a focal point to help us remember what I think Jesus meant us to remember.

Restoring Our Focus

Q. What is it Christ wants us to remember at His Table?

A. He wants us to remember that through the Cross, He completely accomplished His perfect work of salvation, including:

1. *Full justification* for every believer—rendering each of us not only as *forgiven,* but causing each of us to be regarded

in Christ as *never having sinned* at all! (Romans 3:23–26;
4:23–5:2; 8:1–2).

2. *Full dominion* over all the powers of hell—rendering every
bond of soul or spirit *broken,* and bringing deliverance
now from every hellish affliction! (Colossians 2:13–15;
Ephesians 1:18–23; 4:7–8).

3. *Full availability* of healing for every dimension of our
personality—seeing that through His suffering, "by His
stripes you *were* healed!" (Isaiah 53:5; Matthew 8:17;
1 Peter 2:24).

4. *Full release* of God's love—poured forth by His Spirit
to fill our souls with peace as well as to bring recon-
ciling peace and restored unity to strained human
relationships (Romans 5:5; 2 Corinthians 5:15–21;
Ephesians 2:14–17).

Q. How best can we practice "thanksgiving" (the meaning of
eucharist)?

A. We can best display thanksgiving by a prevailing spirit of
praise characterizing the worship we bring to the Lord's
Table. This does not recommend or require a giddiness,
lightness, or irreverence. It does require a reassessment of
tradition and an alteration of any of the morbid, funereal, or
dirge-like habits we have unwittingly allowed to surround
our worship at communion.

Q. What mood ought to characterize the receiving of
communion?

A. A mood of expectancy based on a clear-eyed commemoration of the primary fact central to the communion
table—the *meaning* and *achievement* of His death! In our
remembrance of His dying once-for-all, Christ has *not*
called us to reenact His death but to remember His *triumph!*

"It is finished!" was not a whimpered cry. It is the call from Calvary that echoes across the centuries, down the corridors of hell, and throughout the ramparts of heaven! Jesus is both Lord and Conqueror, and each time we come to His Table we need to remember, and allow faith to fill our hearts for every need we have or circumstance we face!

Q. How can the *worship* at Christ's Table become a *witness* of His power?

A. Worship *and* witness can fill our time at Christ's Table by our employing the observance as an opportunity to *apply* the provisions of Calvary, not simply to remember them. The biblical word "proclaim" underscores a *ministering* of the memorial, not merely an observance thereof. Perhaps this might most be exemplified in the possibilities of seeing people brought to Christ by inviting them to His feast.

A Table-time Invitation

We have found communion worship to be an ideal time for evangelism. That was foreign to my upbringing, and it took a reformation of sorts to release me into such ministry as our "table-time invitation."

First, let me say and emphasize that I feel keenly about, and have always been cautious over, inviting any "as-yet" unbelievers to Christ's Table (1 Corinthians 11:29). However, I began doing it, notwithstanding my caution, because the more I studied the Scriptures, I couldn't find anything prohibiting an unbeliever being *invited* to The Table.

Once I did that, I found *many* being born again there. My predisposition had been against the possibility of opening Christ's Table to overly wide participation. I had grown somehow to see myself as The Table's guardian against unworthy intruders. Any suggestion of an open table was reckless if not heretical, but an important line of discernment changed my perspective.

I began to recognize the vast difference between a sacrilegious person and a searching one—between the indifferent and the inquiring. I became convinced that Jesus would invite the searching heart to partake at His Table, for His own lifestyle and parables support an outreaching viewpoint. He ate with publicans and sinners, never compromising, but ever reaching to them. His parabolic teaching also indicated a wide-openness in God's heart, inviting people to His salvation feast. "all things are ready. Come. ... Go out ... compel them to come in" (Mark 2:16; Matthew 22:4; Luke 14:23). Because of a fresh exposure to God's Word, I abandoned my tradition-fixed fears and I began to preface our congregation's corporate times of communion like this:

"As we come to the Lord's Table today; I want to invite *everyone* who is here to partake with us. Indeed, I want to *urge* you to do so, just as surely as if you were at our house at dinnertime.

"It would be impolite to not at least invite you; however, we're not merely being polite, we honestly want you to share with us. Whatever your religious background or absence of one, you needn't hesitate. You're welcome here. We refuse to close this Table to anyone, because, in fact, it isn't ours.

"This Table is Christ's. He is the One who provided this feast—a feast of forgiveness. He did it when He died to open salvation to us all, and He's the One who calls us all to come here and remember that. His Word is clear: 'Whosoever will may come.'[3]

"I think it is obvious that it would be meaningless and therefore wrong for anyone to partake disrespectfully or indifferently.

However, barring that, let me urge you to come with us. Let us come and thank God for the gift of His Son, and thank His Son for the gift of His life for us."

In such an approach to communion worship, the witness of Jesus' love, life, and power fills the room. At some point *during* the actual time of partaking, I will invite those who "even now are opening your lives toward Jesus" to make a firm decision. It is no wonder that, almost every time we worship at the Lord's Table, there are several first-time respondents who acknowledge Jesus Christ as Savior. Following this, we offer an opportunity to proceed to the prayer room for counseling, and they *do* go— these who actually made their decision *during* the time they were partaking with us.

Our invitation to the unsaved is only one way that His Table may be borne of *witness*. Healing and affirmation are also dynamic possibilities.

The witness of Christ's healing power can be extended in simple faith by allowing believers to obey Jesus' directive: "They will lay hands on the sick, and they will recover" (Mark 16:18). Often when the bread is being partaken, we will pause and restate the verse: "This is my body which is broken for you," noting that Jesus said His physical suffering was specifically *"for"* us—that is, *in our interest*. Just as He died to save us from our sin, He also suffered to obtain and provide relief from our multiplied afflictions.

On these grounds, I encourage worshippers simply to lift a hand to indicate their desire to have nearby worshippers lay hands upon them "in Jesus' Name." We do this without ostentation or religious pomp, as there is a very brief time for those who surround each petitioner to pray over him or her. The results are remarkable and there are regular testimonies of healing that flow from this practice.

Also, what a time this is to love one another!

This is the heart of our witness to the world—the unity of the Body living in the Spirit of Jesus Himself. We nearly always conclude our communion service by rising together, taking time to embrace those around us, and affirm one another in the love and joy of Christ. There is a religious resistance to hugging in church, but this also needs reforming in the light of God's Word. There are no less than five New Testament epistles that *command* all believers to "greet one another with a holy embrace."[4]

The marvel of such meetings as these at His Table is that an electric sense of victory, healing, love, and deliverance fills the room. If the worship of Jesus is central, nothing of irreverence or silliness can creep in. No one is in any danger of forgetting either the price of the Cross or what it purchased. These moments of memorial bring us to remembering what Jesus wanted us to remember, and His people are fed at His Table of triumph.

That was the spirit of the meeting the day Mark was born again.

A five-year-old boy understood, and though it was his dad who gave the explanation on that occasion, whenever God's people understand and communicate Christ's victory, there will be a fresh experience of the same. They will learn again what it means to be a part of His Church, overcoming "through the Blood of the Lamb and the word of their testimony."[5]

Due to his limited experience, my young son had used the word "skin" instead of "body," and his imprecision in terms had brought a chuckle to two adults. However, in another sense, maybe we adults need more of "Jesus' skin" in communion. One wonders if Christ Himself does not desire a reformation in our worship at His Table, one that will let Him "put skin on" His manifest victory by proclaiming that triumph again and again, through and among His people, who celebrate that victory *here and now!*

14

His Majesty Speaks

"Behold, I make all things new!
Believe it, for my words all are true.
And that truth can bring you into liberty—
Behold, I make all things new!"
J.W.H.

There is no reason to doubt the man's testimony. He had proven trustworthy over many years of fellowship and service. However, when someone claims to have seen visions, well, it may understandably make any of us cautious. If he also tells you he saw Jesus, I suppose we all would confess to at least a momentary twinge of skepticism.

However, that's exactly what the man said: "I saw Jesus." He told it this way.

"As you know, vicious and agonizing persecution of Christians had come to our area, and as a result of my stand for Jesus Christ, I was sent to an island penal colony—this particular gulag being not more than 100 miles from my home.

"I had been there for several weeks, feeling nothing unusual other than the loneliness, the lurking sense of depression I suppose any prisoner feels. On this particular day, the guards had allowed us a period of reprieve from our routine of labor, and I had wandered alone to a secluded spot. I sat down on a large stone, facing the sea to the west—the surrounding rocks creating something of a small, chapel-like formation behind me. I was completely without expectation or preparation for what happened, for suddenly I heard a voice. It was so loud I was literally shaken, totally removed from anything approximating a reverie, and that's how I know I wasn't in a trance of some kind. The voice fairly shouted:

> There is nothing that precedes Me and nothing beyond Me! I have always been and will be when time no longer exists. I am here to remove your fears of the future, for I too have been through the pangs of death and the horrors of hell, and I'm here to tell you—all will be well!

"I was stunned, and even while He was speaking I began to turn around. What I saw exceeds description, for even though I knew it was Jesus, I could not have imagined nor can I adequately describe the marvelously transcendent glory of His appearance. Only one word can begin it: *Majestic!*

"His whole being seemed to be infused with light—perhaps *fire* is the better way to state it. A regal garment that seemed to be woven of gold draped to His feet—feet that I can't forget—for though they were without shoes, they shone with an unearthly brilliance. I was surprised that His hair was white, but it wasn't gray as though dimmed by age—it was sheened as though silvered with glory.

"The eyes were unforgettable. They seemed as glowing coals, not of a smoldering, sinister quality, but emanating a warmth, a power, and a penetrating purity of sight that reached into my being when He spoke."

From this point, the man continued his account of what Christ said to him but as the elements of his vision were concerned, that's what he said he saw. Now, having relayed his testimony to you, I wonder what your feeling is about it? I mean, can you accept it at all?

It's probably an unfair question. You're probably the same as I am in such a regard. Even if we allow for the possibility of visions as being real and not imagined, we would both probably reserve judgement until we met the person claiming to have had one.

However, in this particular case, I think you've already passed judgment. I suppose you already believe it, for the report above is actually one you've probably read before in other terms. It was written less than nineteen hundred years ago, and the more commonly read version reads like this:

> I was in the Spirit on the Lord's Day, and I heard
> behind me a loud voice as of a trumpet, saying, "I
> am the Alpha and the Omega, the First and the
> Last … Do not be afraid … I *am* He who lives
> and was dead, and behold, I am alive forevermore.
> Amen. And I have the keys of Hades and of Death.
> Write … the things which will take place after this"
> (Revelation 1:10–19).

With those words, the apostle John writes from the Isle of Patmos, where he was exiled by the Imperial Roman government because of his leadership and influence for the Gospel of Jesus Christ. His narrative of the vision he had of Jesus continues in the Book of Revelation:

> Then I turned to see the voice that spoke with
> me. And having turned I saw seven golden lamp-
> stands, and in the midst of the seven lampstands
> *One* like the Son of Man, clothed with a garment

down to the feet and girded about the chest with
a golden band. His head and hair *were* white like
wool, as white as snow, and His eyes like a flame
of fire; His feet *were* like fine brass, as if refined
in a furnace, and His voice as the sound of many
waters; He had in His right hand seven stars, out
of His mouth went a sharp two-edged sword, and
His countenance *was* like the sun shining in its
strength. And when I saw Him, I fell at His feet as
dead. But He laid His right hand on me, saying to
me, "Do not be afraid; I am the First and the Last"
(Revelation 1:12–17).

There is a reason I have sought to lead you into John's vision by
an apparent detour, as though relating to you some contemporary vision of Christ.

I've done it because I think we need it.

I think we need to remember that Jesus has, in the past,
appeared to people—to stir them afresh with a vision of the
Church as it is and the Church as it can be.

I think we all need a twenty-first-century vision of Jesus
Christ—at least in terms of hearing His call to a new era of conquest unveiled by a new encounter with Him in worship.

Is that credible to you? Or do our traditions disallow us to
have an experience like John had? Does it disturb you as it does
me, that I can comfortably read of John's personal encounter and
not be shattered by its implications for me? That's why I think
we need our own vision.

The object is not sensation seeking, ecstasy or escapism. It's
confrontation—a stark, raw, earth quaking, staggering shake-up
of our senses and our sensitivities, brought through a fresh,

brutally realistic encounter with the King—His Majesty, Jesus—Lord of the Church.

A literary excursion into rephrased history might briefly help us consider the possibility of such a vision, but the real and lasting way to meet and be met by Him is through a more certain and attainable means than seeking our own private visions.

That way is *worship*.

It is worship that is rid of its tameness, its predictability, its numbing formality, and its prison-like expectations of propriety. Such a total and complete upheaval as I need in my own soul will probably never allow for this encounter to take place in public; not because I fear being humbled before others, but because Jesus has a way of dealing with each of us so uniquely that a private setting becomes necessary.

The purpose of such an encounter (and the reason I invite you to join me in such a quest) is that the same realities that took hold of John's soul also grip ours: the reality of Christ's majestic person, the reality of Christ's authoritative position, and the reality of Christ's consummate power.

I am convinced that the Holy Spirit is waiting for hearts that hunger and thirst for an unprecedented visitation of God to our generation—displaying His glorious power and might to every culture and in every church. I am equally convinced that the one pathway to that place is a reformation in the worship life of the Church that is just as dramatic and dynamic as the reformation in the theology of the Church was five centuries ago.

Seeing Jesus' Person

John saw Jesus as He is; the majestic, exalted, enthroned King. Each trait of His personality seems to be emblazoned in the very flesh and sinew of His glorified body that radiated regality and dominion.

I want to look into His eyes and be purified by that fire that waits to surge into me and purge all of me. I want to bow at His feet, not only to touch the marks of ancient wounds, but also to remember that their brasslike character declares His complete qualification to bring every principality and power beneath them.

I want to fall before Him, dead to my self and sin, and alive to receive His authority to minister in His Name.

I want Him to lay His right hand on me, just as He did John. I want Him to so clearly speak His certainty of triumph into my soul, that whatever trial, whatever test, whatever pain, whatever assault of hell I face; however despondent, depressed or despairing I might become under duress of difficulty; I will be steeled against defeat and stand unshakable through His Word.

Hearing Jesus' Voice

John also heard Jesus speak from His position as Lord of the Church, and I bow in His presence to hear those same words again.

1. His message to Ephesus is His call to me: "Come away from the deceptive supposition that doctrinal purity or diligent labor will ever substitute for passionate devotion." The timeless call to us all is "Repent! Return to your first love!" (Revelation 2:1–7).

2. His message to Smyrna is His reminder that my wealth is neither now, nor ever will be, in my accumulation of material things, but in that pure gold of character that flows out of the refining fires of struggle and tribulation—the

trials through which He guarantees to bring me if I will keep tuned to the Spirit's voice (Revelation 2:8–11).

3. His message to Pergamos and Thyatira is His insistence that I give no place to the sensuous and the seductive, which in every age will seek an avenue of justifying carnal indulgence and rationalizing sexual excesses (Revelation 2:12–29).

4. His message to Sardis is His commentary on the shallow human supposition that an established reputation among mankind is in any way impressive to God. The qualifications for recognition on His terms are always the same—a continuously shapeable, teachable, hearing heart that walks in repentant response to the present word the Spirit is speaking to the Church, and a simple walk in faith that overcomes the spirit of the world (Revelation 3:1–6).

5. His message to Philadelphia is His constant encouragement to me. For He never forgets or overlooks my deep desire to please Him, and He promises to open doorways unto my next realm of victory—doors that, once He opens them, no power can resist! (Revelation 3:7–13).

6. His message to Laodicea is His age-long reminder of the vulnerability of my flesh to enshrine success as though gain were God. He calls me from the chilling effect of such blindness and promises to anoint my eyes, clothe my nakedness, and re-fire my soul. He promises to enter the open door of my welcome to Him—"Come in and dine with me, Jesus" (Revelation 3:14–22).

Reformed worship is re-fired worship! It will bring us into Christ's presence to witness His Majesty, and it will bring us to His feet to acknowledge His Lordship.

Experiencing Jesus' Power

John's vision included one more thing. He saw the consummate power of Christ through to the end of all things. The whole Book of Revelation unfolds the message that always and ever, consummately and ultimately, Jesus Christ is Lord and King! He is God triumphant!

With that vision, one wonders if John were drawn back to another day.

The breezes flowing down from Hermon brought a rhythmic sway to the grasses so freshly garbing the Galilean hillsides that spring. The same settings that had witnessed such magnificent, divine grace—the healings, the teachings, the deliverances, the recovery of the broken—all seemed relatively silent now. No crowds were present, but there was a small gathering of almost a dozen men who seemed to be reminiscing on those golden moments of many months now past.

Then He came.

So simply did He arrive, not one of them could be sure if He had slipped up from the flank of their mountaintop situation (*Did He come from the grove of trees over there?*) or if He just appeared miraculously.

> When they saw Him, they worshipped Him; but some doubted. And Jesus came and spoke to them saying, "All authority has been given to Me in heaven and on earth. Go therefore and make disciples of all the nations, baptizing them ... teaching them ...

and lo, I am with you always, *even* to the end of the age" (Matthew 28:17–20).

There's an ineffable glory to this moment, but there is also a distinctly plaintive tone to the text: "They worshipped ... *but some doubted.*"

Some doubted?

Yes ... and so, sometimes, do we.

We need not belabor those men just being birthed into an age mankind could never have imagined. Their doubt occasioned no criticism by the Savior. For He understood the awesome transitions they were being called to accept, the overthrow of presuppositions about *how* Messiah's rule would be extended, as well as their call to be open to a new power source in the Holy Spirit being promised them. It was all so new ... some doubted.

However, they worshipped.

Their dignity, and the release of their destiny, was that they worshipped. So may it be with us. It was unto that worshipping band, and in spite of those lingering doubts that soon would disappear, that Jesus did two things: He commissioned them *and* He conferred divine authority upon them.

> *All* authority has been given to Me. ... you shall
> receive power when the Holy Spirit has come upon
> you ... As the Father has sent Me, I also send you
> (Matthew 28:18; Acts 1:8; John 20:21).

The realm of rule once lost by man was made possible again to the redeemed. God made worshippers recipients of Kingdom authority at Pentecost, to equip them to fulfill His Majesty's call to extend the dominion of His Throne to every person possible until His return.

God calls us in just the same way.

Whatever remains of the present age until He comes again, this much is clear: His Spirit is working in fresh new ways today wherever open hearts are pliable. Today, He no more requires our instant mastery of lingering doubt than He did those early apostles. He only calls us to worship—to offer up all glory, honor, and praise ...

For it is there, as we exalt and lift upon high the Name of His Majesty, that doubts will be scattered like shadows.

For it is there that His power will be outpoured like new wine and that Kingdom authority will flow toward us.

For it is there that Jesus who died, now glorified, will be revealed among us.

So magnify, come glorify Jesus—

Worship His Majesty!

Endnotes

Chapter 2

1. Revelation 12:9 states that Satan, the serpent, and the dragon are one and the same. Jesus not only treats the devil as a personal being and acknowledges his temporary claim to power on this planet (Matthew 4:1–10), but He also speaks of Adam and Eve as being actual people (Matthew 19:4-5). Both facts remove the matter of evil's source and man's beginning and purpose from the realm of mythology or speculation.

Chapter 4

1. Jack Hayford, *The Church On The Way*, chapters 5–8 (Chosen Books, Grand Rapids, 1982).
2. Jack Hayford, *Come O Lord and Overflow Us*, (New Spring, 1982).
3. The attendance figures reflect the total Sunday morning, Sunday night and midweek average attendance for the first half of 1987.

Chapter 7

1. Repeatedly the Lord emphasizes that the priests' ministry will be "unto Me." Examples include Exodus 28:1, 3–4, 41; 29:1, 44; 30:30; 40:13, 15.
2. Ezekiel 40–48 elaborates details of its construction and ministry.

Chapter 8

1. Mrs. F. W Suffield, Public Domain.

Chapter 9

1. It is probably because the death of Eli's sons at the same time as his

left no provision of an adult to assume the role of high priest—a heredi-
tary position.

2. Compare 1 Chronicles 16:7–36 with Psalm 105:1–15, Psalm 96:1–13,
and portions of Psalm 106.

3. Perez–Uzzah.

Chapter 10

1. 1 Corinthians 14:15; 16:1–3; Acts 2:46, 47; 4:24; 20:36; 1 Timothy; 2:8,
4:13–15; Luke 24:50; 2 Timothy 2:15.

2. The joining of "intelligent" and "spiritual" is consistent with the dual
components contained in the words *logiken latre ian*.

Chapter 11

1. "Song-making" and "songwriting" are two entirely different things. I
do not even generally encourage people to think of the songs they sing
spontaneously as songs to be written for others to sing. Of course,
occasionally that will occur, but if the focus of a worship song becomes
songwriting, the pure simplicity of the practice becomes lost in one's
preoccupation with memorability, the effect the song may have on others,
the quality of the melody, the refinement of the lyric, etc. Songwriting
for widespread use is a gift God gives to relatively few; "song-making" is a
gift potential He has given to everyone.

2. Both The Living Bible and the Good News Translation read "sacred
songs," but the New International, New English, New King James,
Revised Standard, Phillips and the older Authorized KJV all translate
to "spiritual songs."

3. Ephesians 5:18-19 directly links our regular refilling with the Holy
Spirit to our exercise in singing.

4. This is actually the composite of two different stories with similar
notes, but the part concerning Aimee personally refers to the same child
throughout.

Chapter 13

1. Greek: *Katangello*, to preach or proclaim.

2. This is obviously what prompts the otherwise confusing final verse in

the passage. Paul directs people to eat at home to answer to hunger's basic need, while the Lord's Table is clearly to be observed with smaller representative portions of the bread and the cup.

3. Revelation 22:17, "And the Spirit and the bride say, 'Come!' And let him who hears say, 'Come!' And let him who thirsts come. Whoever desires, let him take the water of life freely." Matthew 11:28–30, "Come to Me, all *you* who labor and are heavy laden, and I will give you rest. Take My yoke upon you and learn from Me, for I am gentle and lowly in heart, and you will find rest for your souls. For My yoke *is* easy and My burden is light." John 3:16,17, "For God so loved the world that He gave His only begotten Son, that whoever believes in Him should not perish but have everlasting life. For God did not send His Son into the world to condemn the world, but that the world through Him might be saved."

4. Romans 16:16; 1 Corinthians 16:20; 2 Corinthians 13:12; 1 Thessalonians 5:26; 1 Peter 5:14—The oriental "kiss" is a term that has been inclined to preempt our application of a gracious embrace. A hug is the appropriate counterpart in our Western world.

5. The author has written a complete cantata entitled, "The Overcomers," which provides a musical and narrative to communicate this approach to the Lord's Table.

About the Author

Best known affectionately as "Pastor Jack," Dr. Jack Hayford has been experiencing the awesome, miraculous power of God his whole life. He was miraculously healed on two separate occasions, when the medical odds were not in his favor. These life events ignited in him a passion for God and convinced him of the power and presence of the Holy Spirit in the modern church.

Pastor Jack Hayford is the Founding Pastor of The Church on the Way in Van Nuys, California and served as President of The International Church of the Foursquare Gospel from 2004-2009. Pastor Jack serves as the Chandellor of The King's University, which he founded in Los Angeles in 1997.

A prolific and best-selling author, Pastor Jack has written or collaborated on over 100 books and composed over 500 hymns, including the internationally acclaimed hymn "Majesty."

Acknowledged as a bridge-builder across the Body of Christ, Pastor Jack's heart is to bring unity across all denominational and racial boundaries. He is recognized for his balanced teaching, faithful to the undompromising truth of the Bible.

Pastor Jack and his wife, Anna, have four children, eleven grandchildren, and a growing number of great-grandchildren.